basic

ancient truths
for every
christ follower

brad brucker

What people are saying about

We live in a culture of offense that thrives on division and keyboard conflict. *BASIC* is a message of reason that allows the reader (from across tribal lines) to access truth that is common to Jesus-followers. This book is small but potent and presents an engaging overview of seven core doctrines that are central to the Christian faith. Highly recommended!

—Dr. Nate Hettinga, Regional President, Converge Northwest

The Apostle Paul warned Timothy to "watch your life and doctrine closely" (1 Timothy 4:16), and he added "the things you have heard me say in the presence of many witnesses entrust to reliable people who will also be qualified to teach others" (2 Timothy 2:2). In *BASIC*, pastor and author Brad Brucker delineates the core biblical doctrines that we need to learn, live by, and instill in those around us. Read and heed this important book because, as the title says, these truths are for every Christ-follower.

—Mark Mittelberg, Executive Director of the
Lee Strobel Center for Evangelism and Applied Apologetics
at Colorado Christian University (StrobelCenter.com),
and author of *Contagious Faith* **and** *The Questions*
Christians Hope No One Will Ask (With Answers)

Jesus instructs that a wise man builds his house on solid rock. Brucker lays out the foundation for all to easily understand. Whether you are a brand-new follower seeking to build your spiritual life or a veteran in need of a refresh, *BASIC* will ground you in what is most important.

—Bob Black, author of *Mobilize Your Mission,*
Founder of Mission Curve Advisors

What do bumper stickers, sleepwalking, the Avengers, and the Fountain of Youth have in common? They are all illustrations Brad Brucker uses in *BASIC* to explain some of the most asked but rarely answered questions about Christianity. Brucker does an excellent job of tackling the topics of the Bible, the Trinity, the Devil, Salvation, Sin, Hell, and Heaven, plus a few others in an entertaining and informative way. I highly recommend this book to anyone considering the Christian faith.

—JD Pearring, Excel Leadership Network Director

History is speeding up! The book you are holding in your hands points us to a compelling new normal—the ancient and the future reconnected. *BASIC* is a timely, yet foundational and practical discipleship manual for this emerging new normal. You will want to read—and share—this book!

—Dan Serdahl, New Life: People Becoming the Church

Brad Brucker is an amazing servant of the Lord. He is a tireless worker, a great theologian and he has a deep care and concern for helping to equip pastors. Basic is a tremendous resource for all who follow Jesus, especially those who are headed into, or already ministering as a pastor/leaders. I believe that those who read and apply the biblical principles shared in this book will find themselves on track to being extremely fruitful as they seek to build God's kingdom.

Stan Russell, Lead Pastor, Horizon Community Church

As a pastor, one of my greatest desires is to see God's people understand the basic truths of the Christian faith, and for those truths to bring transformation as we become more intimate with God and reach out to others with the love of Jesus. Brad Brucker does an amazing job of bringing those most important truths together in one place. In *BASIC*, Brad challenges the unbeliever to believe, helps the new believer to understand, and reminds the seasoned believer to keep it simple.

—Brett Burner, Pastor, ONE Church, author of
Genuine Faith and *Hand of the Morningstar*

basic
ancient truths for every christ-follower
by brad brucker

Scripture quotations marked (NIV) are taken from The Holy Bible, New International Version®, NIV®. Copyright © 1973, 1978, 1984, 2011 by Biblica, Inc.® Used by Permission of Biblica, Inc.® All rights reserved worldwide.

Scripture quotations marked (NLT) are taken from the Holy Bible, New Living Translation, copyright © 1996, 2004, 2007. Used by permission of Tyndale House Publishers Inc., Carol Stream, Illinois 60188. All rights reserved.

Scripture quotations marked (ESV) are taken from the Holy Bible, English Standard Version, copyright © 2001, 2007, 2011, 2016 by Crossway Bibles, a division of Good News Publishers. Used by permission. All rights reserved.

Scripture quotations marked (NASB) are taken from the New American Standard Bible. Copyright © 1960, 1962, 1963, 1968, 1971, 1972, 1973, 1975, 1977, 1995, 2020 by The Lockman Foundation. A Corporation Not for Profit, La Habra, California. All Rights Reserved.

Published by:

LAMP POST
publishers
www.lamppostpublishers.com

Trade Paperback: ISBN# 978-1-60039-244-3

dedication

For Emmaus—My very first grandchild, whom I desperately love!

You are the personification of where the ancient meets the future! May this book be a guide to ground you in God's word and a light to guide you to The Light— Jesus, your true forever friend!

contents

preface

God spoke to me.

Yeah, I know, it's crazy. "Brad, I want you to build a boat!" Okay, actually, that was Noah. But I sensed in my spirit He was speaking to me. It went something like this:

"Brad, that book *Basic* you are writing… I want to use it to bring my children together. You know Brad, I love them all. I sure want them to love each other. Your book will help."

"Okay, God," I'm thinking, "that's a huge task!"

The next day, as I typically do, I spent some time in the Bible. My Bible reading plan took me to one of my favorite psalms that day—Psalm 121. It's such an astounding psalm. I wrote the first two verses in my journal: "I lift my eyes to the mountains. Where does my help come from? My help comes from the Lord, the Maker of Heaven and earth" (Psalm 121:1-2 NIV). I thought about David or whoever wrote this Psalm. He must have been in a pretty big pickle. *What do I do? How do I deal with this impossible situation?* Then he looks up to the nearby mountains and thinks, "God! God can help me. Yes, God can do it! After all, He made Heaven and Earth!" It's so good! As I thought of the psalmist and his impossible situation, I thought, "Creating Heaven and Earth might be easier than getting your children to love each other, God!"

When I put my faith in Jesus back in 1986 at the age of twenty-eight, I didn't understand why there were so many Christian denominations and why they all just couldn't get along. After studying theology, getting a Master of Divinity degree, and being part of a few different denominations over the years, I understand the "why" of the divisions more. There are various issues at stake. One of those issues is many devout Christ-followers have drifted away from the basics. In Christianity, the most basic "rule," so to speak, is to love God and love others on an increasing basis as we mature in Christ.

Having said this, I pray three things happen to you as a result of reading the book: First, you love God more and you love others more, no matter which Jesus tribe you are connected to. The things that separate us are *not* the core doctrines. It's the other stuff. Though part of different denominations, we all believe in the core, primary or basic doctrines of the Christian faith.

Second, I pray you will recommit yourself to the basics. That's what this book is all about—the basics. Why just the basics? We can get so wrapped up in the secondary doctrines of our tribe or denomination that those doctrines end up dividing us. It's kind of insane. We can disagree on those secondary doctrines, yet still have deep fellowship and even be on mission together when we believe the core doctrines together.

Lastly, I'm concerned. Many people who call themselves Christ-followers have never been taught the basics, or perhaps they have forgotten them. Instead, they often just adopt a belief, a mindset, or an ideology into their own Christianity that really doesn't line up with the historic Christian faith. The writer of Hebrews has a similar concern:

> "You have been believers so long now that you ought to be teaching others. Instead, you need someone to teach you again the basic things about God's word. You are like babies who need milk and cannot eat solid food. For someone who lives on milk is still an infant and doesn't know how to do what is right. Solid food is for those who are mature, who through training have the skill to recognize the difference between right and wrong" (Hebrews 5:12-14 NLT).

The basic things about God's word need to be taught. Why? So, we can all recognize the difference between what's right and what's wrong.

My hope is this book will help you. The Apostle Paul told a young pastor he mentored named Titus, "You, however, must teach what is appropriate to sound doctrine" (Titus 2:1 NIV). In addition to that, Paul wrote to another young pastor named Timothy, "Now the Holy Spirit tells us clearly that in the last times some will turn away from the true faith; they will follow deceptive spirits and teachings that come from demons" (1 Timothy 4:1 NLT). That's kind of scary, but I've seen it all too often. It's one of the main reasons why I'm writing this book. I'm concerned that far too many people, including Christ-followers, are forming their belief system based on the internet, YouTube, the media, politics, friends, the prevailing culture, and even some false teachings in educational institutions—and not on God's word.

Whether you are just starting out on your journey with Jesus or have been a Christ-follower for some time, it is so important that you are able to understand and believe the truths of the basic doctrines deeply and soundly! That's what *Basic* is all about.

introduction

During the 1970s in the United States, a huge scare gripped the parents of trick-or-treating kids like never before. It was reported by many news agencies that razor blades and needles were found in candied apples given to kids while gathering candy (or "sweets" for our African readers) while trick-or-treating in neighborhoods on Halloween. It was riveting! Parents stopped their children from going out to trick-or-treat. Fear for their children paralyzed many parents. That terrifying news radically changed how Halloween was conducted here in the US. But here's the deal: it never happened. It wasn't true!

There were no razor blades or needles found—ever! It became an urban myth that many still believe today, and sadly, no one really questioned it until it was too late. A lie took away a lot of fun, and radically changed the behavior of parents and kids across America. Lies that are believed will ultimately take life *away*. Truth gives life!

Truth! It's a double-edged sword. We have a love-hate relationship with it. Consider for a moment you are not feeling your normal jovial self, and it's been persisting for months. What to do? You go to the doctor hoping it's really nothing, low blood sugar or a minor nutritional deficiency. But you also quietly, yet a bit anxiously, wonder if it's something else, perhaps a heart valve issue or worse—cancer!

Question: If it's the latter, wouldn't you really want to know? If it's early-stage lymphoma and treatable, would you want your doctor to give you the unadulterated truth? Sure, you would! Why? So you could begin the proper treatment, get well, and get back to feeling your good and healthy self as soon as possible. We would all hate to hear the painful truth, but we would be so glad we heard it early enough to treat it. At times like that, truth is our friend. It steers us in the right direction and literally gives us life.

The same is true with spiritual truth. However, many people are increasingly prone to avoid ancient time-tested spiritual truths, or even abandon them altogether. These days, basic truths are much harder to swallow, truths that for centuries have been a given. Maybe it's because they are not taught as consistently as before. Maybe it's because older Christ-followers wrongly assume everyone should know and embrace them. Maybe it's because younger people fear rejection from people they love, and if they were to embrace an unpopular idea or truth they'd be marginalized by their peers. Maybe it's because it's easier to tell people what they want to hear, true or not. (How many times have you accepted some social media post as true only to be directed to Snopes or Factcheck.org and learn it's false? It happens. We need to be a little more careful, don't we?)

For many centuries, the primary arms of the historical Christian church, Catholics, Protestants and the Orthodox church, have largely embraced the ancient creeds that define what a Christ-follower believes. Two of these creeds in particular are very helpful: the Nicene Creed and the Apostles' Creed. Both can be easily found with a quick Google search. For over a thousand years these creeds have been recited regularly in Christian worship services of many denominations to affirm and remind Christ-followers of the primary truths of what Christ-followers believe.

Here's the Apostles' Creed:

I believe in God the Father Almighty,
Maker of Heaven and Earth,
And in Jesus Christ, his only Son our Lord,
Who was conceived by the Holy Ghost,
Born of the Virgin Mary,
Suffered under Pontius Pilate,
Was crucified, dead, and buried.
He descended into hell;
The third day He rose again from the dead;
He ascended into heaven,
And sitteth on the right hand of God the Father
    Almighty;
From thence he shall come to judge the quick
    and the dead.
I believe in the Holy Ghost;
The holy catholic Church, the Communion of
    Saints;[1]
The forgiveness of sins;
The resurrection of the body,
And the life everlasting. Amen.

My goal through this book is to help you understand the basic truths stated in this creed, as well as other primary Christian doctrines, and why they are truths that can be trusted—or not. I will also give you a measuring tool to help you discern my findings on these doctrines.

A few years back, my wife, Ann, and I traveled to Israel with a tour group. There were several buses in our group and each bus had its own guide. Amir, a studied Hebrew man, was our guide. He made it clear right from the start that he was not there simply to tell us what we wanted to hear, but that he would give us the unadulterated truth at every ancient site we toured. He had a grading scale:

A = Absolutely authentic.

B = Maybe authentic but questionable.

C = No way—pretty much all fabricated.

Sometimes he'd add a plus or a minus to the grade for flare. To be honest, at first, when we came upon a "B" site it was a bit disconcerting. For example, on the morning of our first full day in Israel, we were in Nazareth, Jesus' hometown, and went up to the Mount of Precipice, the traditional site where an angry mob sought to throw Jesus off a cliff (Luke 4:28-30). Amir, with no qualms, gave the site a B minus. My wife and I were a bit bummed. "Really, Amir?" I thought. "This guide is going to decimate our trip to the ancient ruins!"

But over the course of six days, I very much came to appreciate Amir's insight, wisdom, and candor. In fact, on day six we toured Bethlehem, which was inside the West Bank where Palestinians reside. At the gate into the West Bank, Amir, being an Israeli Jew, was not allowed to enter and had to get off the bus, and another guide, Jeru², took Amir's place. Now, Jeru was a great guy, but it became clear early on in Bethlehem that Jeru just parroted the local tourist story that sold. He told us everything we wanted to hear, and most of the forty-plus people on our bus were woefully disappointed in that part of the tour. After that day, to a person, we all had a new and heightened appreciation for Amir. We couldn't wait to have him back in our bus! Truth, honesty, and wisdom are so refreshing. Sometimes you just don't know what you've got until it's gone.

Sometimes in life, and even in the Church, our "tour bus" has been hijacked by a guide who just wants to tell us what feels good. So please allow me to be your "Amir" through this little book. It is my hope and desire to present to you the basic ancient truths of the historical Christian faith.

Minor on the Minors and Major on the Majors

In America, even in Christian circles, many people have lost or never been taught the historical basic truths or doctrines of our faith. Can you believe it?

Doctrine. That can be a scary word, but don't let that word intimidate you. *Doctrine* simply means *teaching.* Generally, when it comes to religion or religious groups, doctrine is an *important teaching* of that group or organization. Through this book, my mission is to present to you the *primary* or *major* doctrines of the Christian faith in a way you can understand them, embrace them, and apply them as you grow in your relationship with God. As alluded to above, there are both *major* doctrines (basics) and *minor* doctrines (secondary). The majors are generally what all Christian denominations would agree on. For example, in Chapter Two I cover the primary doctrine of the Holy Trinity. If you are a Christ-follower, it's vital to believe in and embrace the Holy Trinity. The minor doctrines would include such teachings as water baptism, communion, head coverings, etc., including how they are interpreted and administered. This book is *all about the majors* and *not about the minors.* Not that those minor doctrines aren't important—they are. But I was taught in seminary to major on the majors and minor on the minors. This mindset has helped me truly love passionate Christ-followers who are adamant about their denominational position on a minor doctrine on which I may not be in agreement. We can still love each other deeply, have fellowship, and even be on mission together.

What if Christ-followers of every tribe/denomination could come together and have a genuine love for each other because they understand the majors? It's the minors that often divide us. That's often how churches split and how whole denominations are started. Yes, God even uses those splits or divisions to accomplish His purposes. But just as often, it causes one Christ-follower to hate another. I am convinced by all that Jesus and the Scriptures have taught that God wants us to truly love each other. That is a key reason I believe God wanted me to write this book.

In this book are the basic truths of the Christian faith. If you and your children understand and embrace these seven truths, you will find that your behavior will become radically changed—about God, about life, about the hope of Heaven, directing you to experience more love, more joy, and frankly, more fun, while reaching more and more people for Jesus. These truths will help you discern between what is true and false, especially regarding issues of faith. I mean, it's pretty messy out there! Sometimes even longtime self-professed Christians hold some wild "razor blades in candied apples" beliefs about our faith that are not healthy, untruths which they pass on to others and defend with self-righteous anger. More than ever, we need to know what is biblical truth.

The format for presenting these truths is through facts, scripture, story, and how each truth can become vitally meaningful to your life and existence. They are that important! Know that some are bound to rub you the wrong way and may even seem offensive in the light of the ideals professed in popular culture. I simply ask that you let the truth speak for itself and stay with me—all the way through each chapter. You'll be glad you did.

Let's jump in!

basic

one

The Bible

When we buy a new car or computer or even a new smartphone, they come with an owner's manual. Most big purchases do. But whatever the price of our material acquisitions, the value of a human being is much greater. We are so valuable to our Maker, you would think each human would come with an owner's manual. Well, we do! It's called the Bible. Unfortunately, like a car owner's manual that gets tucked away in the glove box and never looked at, many Bibles end up on a shelf or in a closet for years and are never read. That's a shame, because the Bible offers amazing insights into how to make the most out of life and really live as our Maker intended.

But Is the Bible True?

This is a great question. After all, the Bible is *so* old. How can it be true when it's been translated and paraphrased over and over and over again for centuries? There is no way it can be accurate to what was written way back two or three thousand years ago, right? Wrong! The Bible was written over a period of about 1500 years (around 1400 BC to about 100 AD) by approximately forty human authors, inspired by the Holy Spirit (I will expound on the Holy Spirit in the next chapter—just trust me for now). Good translations of the Bible are not "retranslated or paraphrased over and over again." The best translations are done in a very systematic and scholarly fashion. Teams of translators go back to the oldest and most difficult readings of the ancient fragments and manuscripts and translate directly from those documents.

Fragments and Manuscripts

The Old Testament was originally written in Hebrew and some Aramaic, while the New Testament was originally written in Koine Greek. We have zero original *autographs* or "original" scrolls or fragments of manuscripts of the books of the Bible. Originals are called autographs by all those smart researchers and theologians who study and defend these matters. Everything that has been dug up or found is a copy of some sort. That seems to be bad news, doesn't it?

Scholars didn't have much in the way of fragments or manuscripts of the Old Testament Hebrew Bible that dated much earlier than 1000 AD—until 1946 when the Dead Sea Scrolls were discovered at Qumran by Bedouin shepherds and archaeologists. The Dead Sea Scroll discovery was remarkable. Some scrolls were dated back to around 200 BC, and many were incredibly close to what we had from 1000 years later. For example, "One scholar observed that two copies of Isaiah found in the Qumran caves, 'proved to be word for word identical with our standard Hebrew Bible in more than 95 percent of the text.'"[3]

The New Testament has many, *many* ancient Greek fragments and manuscripts from different dates and places. There have been 5,664 ancient Greek New Testament manuscripts found.[4] That's exponentially more than *any other writing* from virtually any ancient time period. Some are dated back as early as 100 AD to 150 AD. Remember, Jesus lived from about 3 BC to about 30 AD before He was crucified. Some of Jesus' apostles and New Testament writers likely lived to close to 90 or 100 AD, making the date of some of those manuscripts very close to the time of their original writing.

History and Archaeology

Many skeptics have tried to disprove the truth of the Bible over the centuries, only to have an archaeological discovery happen that destroyed their "skeptical theory." One such skeptic was Sir William Ramsey. He was an esteemed Oxford atheist and archaeologist who lived in the nineteenth century. He embarked on a twenty-five-year journey to disprove the Bible and specifically focused on the book of Acts, written by Luke, a physician, who was also the writer of the Gospel of Luke and travel companion of the Apostle Paul. Ramsey cataloged the Apostle Paul's missionary journeys around the Mediterranean as written by Luke in Acts. After over twenty years of archaeological digs and study, Sir William Ramsey declared, "Luke is a historian of the first rank; this author should be placed along with the very greatest of historians." And later Ramsey sent shockwaves through the academic world by declaring himself a Christian.[5]

What's amazing about Sir William Ramsey is he had an open mind. Many secular teachers and professors in our universities across America simply don't. In philosophy classes especially, some teachers throw statements out to impressionable young students like, "The Bible is nothing but a bunch of fairy tales," without offering any defensible reasons as to why they might say that. And then, if they are challenged by a student, they mock or somehow discredit, marginalize, and cancel that student. It's shameful!

Here's the truth about the Bible: The Bible is, by far, the most scrutinized body of literature in human history. The Bible has stood the test of time. Year after year, for many centuries now, the Bible has stood alone on top of the all-time bestsellers list. In fact, it's way above all the number ones on the *New York Times* bestseller list. Nothing in the Bible has ever been overturned by an archaeological find. On the contrary, archeology continues to affirm facts and coinage, towns, and historical aspects that are written in the Bible. I had a professor in seminary who often went to the holy land on archaeological digs who said this about the Bible: *"We didn't make it up, we dug it up!"*

Which Bible Translation Is a Good One?

There are many good translations of the Bible. The *New International Version* (NIV), the *New Living Translation* (NLT), the *New American Standard Version* (NASB), the *New Revised Standard Version* (NRSV), and the *New King James Version* (NKJV) are just a few. The key to finding a good translation is to determine if it's a *translation* or a *paraphrase*. Paraphrased versions like *The Message Bible* can be helpful, but they are actually retooled words from a recent English translation. The most accurate Bible translations are done by teams of translators who go all the way back to the ancient Hebrew, Aramaic, and Greek fragments and manuscripts as their sources. When choosing a Bible, you will find a more accurate representation of the original biblical text by choosing a translation over a paraphrase.

Inerrancy and Inspiration

If the Bible is true, it can be trusted. Most devoted Christ-followers believe that the Bible is *inerrant* in its original autographs. Inerrant means that when the Bible was originally written by God's chosen servants who carefully wrote down only what the Holy Spirit inspired, that writing was produced without error. Here's what one of those inspired writers wrote:

> "All Scripture is inspired by God and is useful to teach us what is true and to make us realize what is wrong in our lives. It corrects us when we are wrong and teaches us to do what is right" (2 Timothy 3:16 NLT).

Pretty wild, huh? Now you may ask, did God audibly dictate to these human writers exactly what to write down, or did He put a teleprompter in the sky or on their eyelids as they prayed? Sometimes perhaps, like when Moses received the Ten Commandments. But historic Christianity believes the Holy Spirit breathed the words of the Bible into the human writers in a supernatural way that was far greater than me being inspired to write this book, or any other author who has been inspired to write any book. Let's put it this way: the Bible writers were *Inspired*—with a capital "I". And while other writers of other books certainly can be inspired, it is always with a small "i". That probably doesn't clear everything up for you, but as you will see in the next chapter, we can't totally figure out exactly how God does everything. Some things He does are a bit of a mystery. After all, He is God! The one amazing thing most Christian scholars agree on is that God inspired both men and women, using their unique personalities, situations, and even their sins and messy lives to write the Bible—and every word *in* the Bible—as *His* word.

> "The word of God is alive and active. Sharper than any double-edged sword, it penetrates even to dividing soul and spirit, joints and marrow; it judges the thoughts and attitudes of the heart" (Hebrews 4:12 NIV).

That means the Bible has the power to radically transform your life if you desire to learn it and follow it. The Bible will become your filter through which you strain all other information and "truths." If there is something you hear, see, or read, it's wise to go to the Bible to check if aligns with God's word. If it does, keep it. If not, throw it away.

In the next chapter on the Holy Trinity, you will learn that God is a very personal God and longs to have a relationship with us—with *you*! One of the most powerful ways to develop a relationship with God is by reading and living out His word. The Bible is His love letter to us. We need to interpret the Bible through the lenses of love. Jesus gives a great lesson to help us interpret Scripture that, unfortunately, many well-meaning Christians over the centuries didn't get. Jesus was asked by a religious expert what the greatest commandments in Scripture were.

> "Jesus replied, '"Love the Lord your God with all your heart and with all your soul and with all your mind." This is the first and greatest commandment. And the second is like it; "Love your neighbor as yourself." All the Law and the Prophets hang on these two commandments'" (Matthew 22:37-40 NIV).

In that last phrase, Jesus was saying the whole Bible was written for two reasons: to love God and love people. Loving our neighbor proves how much we love God. Loving God and loving people are the lenses through which we must interpret all of Scripture. If we don't have that framework, we are in danger of abusing or manipulating people for our own purposes with the very Word of God. But if we put on our "love lenses" as we read and live out His word, we will develop a deep and abiding relationship with the God of the universe. That is why I encourage people everywhere to spend time with God in prayer and to spend time with God as they read and reflect on Scripture. Read it as if a loving father is speaking it directly to you. Take His words deep into your soul.

Several years ago, my daughter, Sarah, went off to Australia to spend two years at a college there. I was excited for her, but even more excited for myself—at long last I had the opportunity to go to Australia to check off my number one Bucket List item: dive the Great Barrier Reef. So, after a year of her schooling, my wife sent me off for a two-week vacation to visit Sarah. I made all the plans, secured a hotel in Sydney, found a dive shop in Cairns to get our diving certification, and off I went. We spent a few days in Sydney together and then flew to Cairns. I was so excited, finally my dream to explore the expanse and wonder of the Great Barrier Reef would come true. It didn't take me long to realize the extra bonus God had afforded me: to do it with Sarah. What a joy! We had so much fun. After we enjoyed three days and two nights on a live-aboard boat diving the reef, we spent our last night in Cairns, having a ball.

Something happened to me Down Under that was more important than checking off my top Bucket List item. During that last night it dawned on me that after twenty years of being Sarah's father, my goal of parenting had been realized. Sarah and I had become best friends. When the day came to head back to Oregon, I met Sarah at my hotel a few blocks away from her college campus, I walked her to the corner, and we said goodbye. It hit me like never before, tears welled up in my eyes, and I already missed her. Just the thought of leaving her in Australia with the entire Pacific Ocean and an equator separating us made me long for her. Within days, once again, my heart ached to see her, to be with her again. Why? Love. We had, and still have, a deep abiding relationship.

Over the years, I have come to realize a similar phenomenon with God. To date, I've been reading my Bible and journaling and meditating on Scripture daily for over twenty-five years. To be sure, there are days I have skipped my Bible reading and journaling, but when that happens, I soon discover that I am missing Him. Why? Love. It's been said that God has no favorites, just *intimates*. Jesus was the model for what it is to be the Father's intimate, and God desires each of us to be intimates too. I have chosen to live as one of his intimates, and anyone can become one. The Lord longs for intimacy and deep friendship with all His children. God is ready. We have a role to fulfill, and a big part of our role happens when we spend time with Him by praying and reading the Bible daily.

Jesus prioritized His intimate time with the Father. "Before daybreak the next morning, Jesus got up and went out to an isolated place to pray" (Mark 1:35 NLT). Time and again, Jesus placed a huge value on spending quiet time with the Father. I'm convinced Jesus loved to spend time with His Father and knew it was essential to His purpose and mission on this earth. We need to ask ourselves: if Jesus needed to spend regular quiet time with the Father, how much more do we?[6]

Charles Haddon Spurgeon, who lived in the nineteenth century and was one of the wisest and greatest preachers in recent modern history, said this about the Bible: "Many books in my library are now behind and beneath me. They were good in their way once, and so were the clothes I wore when I was ten years old, but I have outgrown them; Nobody ever outgrows Scripture; the book widens and deepens with our years."[7]

Where is the Bible on Amir's scale?

A = Absolutely authentic.

B = Maybe authentic but questionable.

C = No way—pretty much all fabricated.

The Bible is absolutely true, and it has changed more lives than all other books written put together. It's an "A" all the way on Amir's scale!

God Revealing Himself in Scripture Changed Everything

Ever since humans populated the earth, many cultures worshiped a creator God of some sort, but it wasn't until God decided to reveal Himself intimately to Abraham, Isaac, and Jacob, and then even more so to Moses, that humanity could begin to understand the all-knowing, all-loving, omnipotent, omnipresent nature of God.

The fact that God had Moses write the first five books of the Bible and then reveal Himself to the prophets, the psalmists, and historical writers is astounding. No other people had ever been given such a deep understanding of God before.

The icing on the cake, so to speak, is that God would become incarnate—take on human flesh—in Jesus. That act of God even blew the minds of angels (1 Peter 1:12). The Passion of Christ, his going to the cross to pay for the sins of humanity, ultimately would reveal the depth of God's love in an unspeakable way. Never before had such a god been known to humankind.

All this and more were cataloged by the writers of Holy Scripture under the inspiration and guidance of the Holy Spirit.

It's clear God longs to have a beautiful, loving, and intimate relationship with every human being. Every person who can get their hands on a Bible has the equal opportunity to become one of God's intimates. Will you?

If you long to be the person God has created you to be, read the Bible. Study the Bible. Live out the Bible as if it is a hundred percent true—because it is! Make it your life-long goal. This old quip rings true, *"Show me a person whose Bible is falling apart, and I show you a person whose life is pretty well together."* But be careful, it's also been said, *"It's not so important that you get through the Bible as the Bible gets through you."*

Next, we'll dive into the mystery of the Godhead—the Holy Trinity.

two

The Holy Trinity

When I first became a Christian and was looking for a church to attend, a Catholic friend directed me to a great non-Catholic church in Seattle. He said, "Whatever church you attend, make sure it believes in the Holy Trinity." That was the best advice I could have ever received back then. I offer the same advice to you right now. Let the doctrine of the Trinity be your guiding light when forming a church or selecting a church to attend. It's like when you offer a cashier a hundred dollar bill. They hold it up to the light to look for fibers or a hologram in the bill to determine if it's real or counterfeit. The Holy Trinity is the hologram of the Christian faith. Whether or not a church believes in the Holy Trinity will most often define its authenticity as a truly Christian church.

The teaching of the Holy Trinity is perhaps the most important doctrine of the Christian faith, and perhaps the most mysterious.

The most important because everything we believe flows from the Holy Trinity. The most mysterious because in using the verbiage of the Trinity, we as finite human beings are simply attempting to explain our infinite God. And, if we're honest, we can only go as far as the Bible allows us to go.

Before I get too far, here's one thing you need to know about the Holy Trinity. The word *Trinity* isn't even in the Bible. But neither is the word *Bible*. Well, what then? As before, bear with me for a bit and I promise a clear explanation!

The word trinity means *tri-unity*, or "three, yet one." Historic Christianity believes God is made up of three distinct divine persons—the Father, the Son, and the Holy Spirit. Each is eternal and has existed for *all* eternity—past, present, and future—and are a hundred percent unified in who They are and what They do. Using analogies to explain the Trinity is difficult but let me give it a shot. Take the United States of America: we are fifty distinct states, yet one country. Where that analogy breaks down is in social philosophy. California does not even come close to believing what Texas believes on many social issues, whereas the Father, Son, and Holy Spirit are entirely on the same page on everything and are all equally God. They do, however, perform different functions—we'll get to that soon.

Not Modalism

One big mistake theologians and scholars have made in trying to explain the Trinity is using bad analogies. One bad analogy is water. They say, "In thinking of God, consider as though sometimes He is water, sometimes He is ice, and sometimes He is steam." It is all water, they say, just different *modes* of water. That is an ancient *heresy* about God. Yes, I called this analogy a heresy.

Think of heresy as kind of like "fake news"—it is very deceptive and believing a heresy will get a person way off track. The heresy of God showing up in different modes is called *modalism*—"Sometimes God is the Father, sometimes God is the Son, and sometimes God is the Holy Spirit," the modalist proclaims. It seems like no big deal, but it's like saying sometimes Texas is California. When the Bible says the two become one when we get married, does that mean we have literally become one person, and sometimes I manifest myself as the husband, and sometimes I manifest myself as the wife? Absolutely not! My wife and I have become one through marriage, and, ideally, we are unified in approaching life and faith issues, but we are also still distinctively different persons, existing simultaneously. That's how it is with the Holy Trinity. And the fact that God exists in the *personhood* of the Trinity means we can have a deep personal relationship with God. No other religion allows for that.

One other important understanding of the Holy Trinity is *God Substance*. For a few centuries in the early church, the doctrine of the Holy Trinity came under attack. Then in 325AD, a church leadership conference was held called the Council of Nicaea, and another was held in 381AD called the Council of Constantinople. Here is the short version of what came out of both councils: it was decided that God the Father, God the Son, and God the Holy Spirit were all of the same *nature* and *substance*. What also happened is that some heresies which disagreed with the Holy Trinity were exposed and debunked. One of the biggest problems in these councils was determining *who Jesus was*. Was He really *fully God* and *fully man?* How can this be? They were trying to comprehend the mystery! The following is part of one verse of the Bible that affirms this key truth about Jesus Christ being God:

> "Who, being in the very nature God..." (Philippians 2:6 NIV)

This one phrase was a part of an ancient song which many scholars believe was sung regularly in Christian worship back in days of the early church. The Apostle Paul, inspired by the Holy Spirit, gathered up that verse, wrote it down, and made it part of the Holy Scripture.

During the Council of Nicea, as these early Christian leaders struggled to understand and convey how Jesus, God's Son, was also fully God, they used the key word *homoousios* as defined in what would become the Nicene Creed as follows:

> **Homoousios – Greek: "of one substance" –** in Christianity, the key term of the Christological Doctrine formulated at the first ecumenical council, held at Nicaea in 325 AD, to affirm that God the Son and God the Father are of the same substance.[8]

The first part of the Nicene Creed reads as follows:

> "I believe in one God,
> the Father almighty,
> maker of heaven and earth,

of all things visible and invisible.
I believe in one Lord Jesus Christ,
the Only Begotten Son of God,
born of the Father before all ages.
God from God, Light from Light,
true God from true God,
begotten, not made, consubstantial*

[*homoousios = One Substance]

with the Father;
through him all things were made."

The divine persons of the Holy Trinity are of the same "God" nature and "God" substance, equal in every way yet performing different God roles. But all the roles we see make God very personal. Let's look at some scriptures which clearly show the personal nature of the Holy Trinity.

In the second verse of the Bible, in Genesis, it says, "…the Spirit of God was hovering over the waters" (Genesis 1:2 NIV). The Holy Spirit was intimately involved in creation, but so was the Son. In John 1:3 the Bible says, "Through him [Jesus] all things were made; without him nothing was made that has been made" (John 1:3 NIV).

Why did God create the heavens and the earth and everything else? In Revelation 4 it says, "For you created all things and they exist because you created what you pleased" (Revelation 4:11b NIV). Some interpreters have flipped the last two words, interpreting the verse to read. "You created what pleased you," or "for Your pleasure" they were created. And we know much of what pleases God was created for you and me! Humanity is the crown of His creation. What we see, feel, touch, and enjoy in this world is a huge gift from God to us! After God created the world in Genesis chapter 1, He then created humankind. Look very carefully at this verse:

> "Then God said, 'Let *us* make mankind in *our* image, *our* likeness...'" (Genesis 1:26a NIV, *italics added*).

Notice the words *us*, *our*, and *our*. Would God use "us" and "our" if He existed alone? Rather, I believe that the Son and the Holy Spirit were with him, and that this verse declares a clear reference to the Holy Trinity. Further, the fact that God made humanity in His image and likeness shows the personal nature of God and His desire to have a deeply personal relationship with each and every human being.

That said, we do need to be careful. We are indeed made in His image, but consider this: Imagine if I were to show you a picture of my son, Nathan, and I asked you, "Is that my son?" Assuming you knew him, you would probably say, "Yes, that's your son." To which I would reply, "No, that's not my son. That's merely a picture, an image of my son." Get it? Human beings will never be of the *same substance* and nature as God. God will always be the creator, and we will always be His creation. What's amazing about the Trinity is that as we pray, worship, and interact with God in Scripture and in life, we can get to know each person of the Holy Trinity intimately. This enables us to reflect His image more closely and bring glory to God, which gives Him great pleasure and gives us the greatest sense of purpose. *Imago Dei* is the Latin for "Image of God." You are made in the Imago Dei! Remember to protect it, knowing that the Devil hates it and will do everything to destroy the Imago Dei in you. We will discuss more on that in upcoming chapters.

Before I get into each person of the Holy Trinity, think about this: Have you ever wondered why we are so enamored with superheroes? I love Superman, Spider-Man, Iron Man, the Hulk, Thor, Captain America, and Wonder Woman. They're all great! It's amazing to me that Hollywood creates them all, and I think I know why. I believe, unknown to most comic authors, screenwriters, and producers, they all have a deep longing for some sort of relationship with God. Think about it. Each one of the superhero characters is awesome. Each one has a distinct personality, and sometimes in the script, they or their evil nemesis are referred to as a god. The big difference between our Hollywood-created superheroes and the Trinity is that the superheroes are fictional, but God is real. Ironically, most of humanity will never ever know any of the superheroes or the actors who play them, but we can know each person of the Holy Trinity intimately.

God the Father

There are specific God-roles within the Holy Trinity. For example, it seems God the Father planned creation and actually spoke it into being. God the Father appears to be the Grand Designer and Architect of the entire cosmos. Even the scientific community is amazed by how everything in the observable realm of our universe seems to be perfectly designed and ultra-fine-tuned to support human life on earth. I would even go as far as to say, not only designed to simply support human life, but designed to make it thrive. Compared to any other planet or sphere in the sky, Earth is an utterly amazing paradise, because it was designed that way by a very good Father.

Some have depicted the God of the Old Testament to be an ancient, angry, distant deity with long white hair and a flowing beard who sits somewhere in the heavens and cares less about humanity and more about maintaining his authoritarian image. That sounds a bit like Cecil B. DeMille's movie *The Ten Commandments*, when Charlton Heston played Moses in 1956. Although I loved the movie, I can see how more than a few people may hold that perspective of God the Father.

In his fascinating book *Faith of The Fatherless: The Psychology of Atheism*, Paul Vitz provides amazing insight into why and how atheists become atheists. The relationship between our earthly father and our Heavenly Father plays an enormous role and is undeniable. Often our view of our Heavenly Father is significantly formed by our interactions and experiences with our earthy father. It's quite remarkable. If our earthy father was distant, that's what we believe about our Heavenly Father. If our earthy father was absent physically and/or emotionally, that can easily be our misperception of God the Father. In fact, this is often where atheists form their beliefs. If their earthy father died or was simply gone or very emotionally abusive, they may come to totally dismiss the existence of a Heavenly Father.[9]

Many former atheists have overcome the misgivings of their earthly fathers by looking to the Bible to forgive their fathers and reframe their view of God the Father. Here's a verse that can be a great help:

> "A father to the fatherless, a defender of the widows, is God in his holy dwelling. God sets the lonely in families, he leads out the prisoners with singing..." (Psalm 68:5-6 NIV).

Wow! That's the Old Testament God the Father—a father to the fatherless, who is incredibly compassionate and loving. He cares deeply for all who are oppressed. He's a champion of the fatherless and widows.

There are many more verses in the Old Testament that show how wonderful our Heavenly Father is—too many for this book. Even as His children rebel against Him, He still shows love and kindness. The prophet Jeremiah records the words of God the Father:

> "I said to myself, 'How gladly would I treat you like my children and give you a pleasant land, the most beautiful inheritance of any nation.' I thought you would call me 'Father' and not turn away from following me" (Jeremiah 3:19 NIV).

This verse shows how painful it is for God the Father to watch His children turn away. He longed for a deep loving relationship with His children, the people of Israel. Yet even after He gave them everything, they turned their back on Him. Who became angry and distant here? Like a rebellious teen who gives his loving parents

the finger as he slams the door of their home in a huff, the people of Israel abandoned God the Father, time and again. But He
always sought to reconcile and provide a way back for them. Why?
Relationship. He loved them no matter what. And He loves you no
matter what. That's why He sent His Son to this world.

God the Son

God the Son has existed for all eternity. In the Gospel of John, we
read, "In the beginning was the Word and the Word was with God
and the Word was God" (John 1:1 NIV). *The Word* John is talking
about is the Son, who became the man, Jesus. This becomes quite
apparent a few verses later, "The Word became flesh and made his
dwelling among us. We have seen his glory, the glory of the one
and only Son, who came from the Father, full of grace and truth"
(1:14). The New Testament makes it clear that Jesus became fully
man, but also remained fully God. Some theologians call Him the
God-Man! That works for me.

The Virgin Birth

The Word became flesh in the most miraculous way. The
Gospel of Luke tells us that the virgin Mary conceived not through
intimacy with a man, but through God's power. When told by
the angel Gabriel that she would give birth to the Son of God and
name him "Jesus," the Bible reveals the following:

> "Mary asked the angel, 'But how can this hap-
> pen? I am a virgin.' The angel replied, 'The Holy

Spirit will come upon you, and the power of the
Most High will overshadow you. So, the baby to
be born will be holy, and he will be called the Son
of God'" (Luke 1:35 NLT).

The virgin birth is a primary doctrine of the historic Christian
Church. But sometimes, in seeking to understand it, people get
confused. "How can this happen?" people ask. My answer to that
question is, logically, if God created the heavens and the earth, don't
you think He could add a holy Y chromosome to an X chromosome in an egg in Mary's womb to make her pregnant with a son?
That seems like literal child's play for God. Then other well-meaning Christians who seek to explain how Mary got pregnant misin-
terpret the above verses and say God had sex with her—which is
completely off base. That is the stuff of mythical cults and pagan
religions: "The gods had sex with humans." That is absolutely not
what happened when Mary became pregnant with Jesus, and it is a
misinterpretation of Scripture to say so. It simply was and is a great
and awesome miracle performed by God through the Holy Spirit.
Believe it.

Identifying the Son

Some religions believe Jesus was a great man and teacher. Some,
like the Mormon faith, believe he was a very good man who, by obe-
diently doing all that God the Father asked of Him, *became* a god,
the god of His own planet. And they say if you do all that their faith
system prescribes, *you too* can become a god of your own planet, but
only if you're a man. If you're a woman, you can't. A simplified role

of females in Mormonism is to be eternally pregnant and populate the planet your husband is the god of. I know, it sounds a little weird, right? Generally, when it comes to spiritual things, if it's weird, it could be a red or yellow flag. Proceed with caution.

The crux of the matter with Jesus is this: True Christianity believes that God became a man, *not* that man became, or becomes, a god. Do you see the difference? Too many men in human history have thought themselves to be gods. It's called the *messiah syndrome*. It's a superego run riot that causes humanity all sorts of damage. It's been said that the only person who never had any element of the messiah syndrome was the only true Messiah, Jesus.

The Role of the Son

What's the role of the Son in the Holy Trinity? Well, if the Father is the Grand Designer and Architect, God the Son is the Builder. "Through Him all things were made; without him nothing was made that has been made" (John 1:3 NIV). He is also the catalyst for redemption, reconstruction, and restoration. The Apostle Paul wrote to the church in Colossae and said this about the Son:

> "The Son is the image of the invisible God, the firstborn over all creation. For in Him all things were created: things in Heaven and on earth, visible and invisible, whether thrones or powers or rulers or authorities; all things have been created through him and for him. He is before all things, and in him all things hold together" (Colossians 1:15-17 NIV).

Just ponder that for a few minutes, and don't get hung up on the word *firstborn*. Sometimes our understanding of English words can confuse the meaning of the original Bible writers. Paul is not saying the Son was born in the Heavens somewhere—and he's *not* saying God the Father had a baby son. While Jesus was born as a human baby, that is not what this passage is referring to by *firstborn*. This is when those really smart Bible scholars are very helpful: "In the Old Testament '*firstborn*' occurs 130 times to describe one who is supreme. It also refers to the one who had a special place in the Father's love."[10] So as it is used here in Colossians 1, the word *firstborn* has nothing to do with a person being born. It does have everything to do with Jesus being first, or supreme, in all things.

The central role the Son played in the Holy Trinity came after He took on the flesh of a human being. He lived a perfect life and taught humanity how to be the very best human beings we can be. He was and is a splendid model to follow, but His primary role was to die on the cross to pay the penalty for your sins and mine. This is called atonement.

Atonement Theories

In Christianity, the word *atonement* comes from the sixteenth century idea of being "at one-ment," meaning to be "in harmony," or reconciled, to God. Because of sin, we are out of harmony with God, and in order us to be reconciled in our relationship with the Father, sin must be dealt with by paying the penalty for our wrongdoing. When Jesus died on the cross he provided atonement, personally paying the price for our sins, restoring our relationship with God. But who gets paid, God or the Devil?

The **Ransom Theory of Atonement** says when we sin, we belong to the Devil until he is paid off. This would mean that when Jesus died on the cross, the Devil was paid with the life of Jesus. This theory grew in popularity when the great Christian writer C.S. Lewis wrote the book *The Lion, the Witch and the Wardrobe.*

As the story goes, the White Witch (representing the Devil) deceives Edmund, bringing him under her spell and coercing him to betray his family and the people of the land of Narnia. When Aslan, the Great Lion (personifying Jesus), learns of Edmund's treachery, he meets with the White Witch to discuss the terms of Edmund's release. The stakes are high! It appears that Aslan must give up his life on the stone table (representing the cross) as payment to the White Witch to secure Edmund's freedom.

Even though *The Lion, the Witch and the Wardrobe* is a children's tale, many in Christendom saw this as an opportunity to take aim at Lewis for heretically teaching and encouraging Ransom Theory. However, Lewis never embraced it as his personal theological view. In fact, even though the story seems to be a representation of Ransom Theory, further inspection reveals something altogether different. When Aslan meets with the White Witch to discuss the terms of Edmund's release, the White Witch says about Edmund, "You have a traitor there, Aslan," to which Aslan replies, "Well, his offense is not against you."[11] Edmund's sin was against God. Aslan laying his life down for Edmund was not to pay the White Witch, it was to pay the Lord. This leads us to the second theory of atonement: *Penal Substitution.*

Penal Substitution says the penalty for sin needs to be paid, but we are spiritually bankrupt and can't pay it. Therefore, God sent

His Son to be a substitute for us, to die in our place. Sin needs to be atoned for. Reparation needs to be paid and the payment is due to God and God alone.

David understood this when he sinned by committing adultery with Bathsheba and having her husband, Uriah the Hittite, killed. In Psalm 51:4a he cried out to God, "Against you, you alone have I sinned; I have done what is evil in your sight" (NIV). David understood that his sin was not against Bathsheba, or Uriah, but against God. His sin needed to be atoned for. *All* our sins need to be atoned for. For David, he had a forward-looking faith in a coming Messiah who would atone for our sins. For us, Jesus is in the rearview mirror. We look back and see that Jesus has already paid the penalty for our sins.

Many Bible verses point to Jesus dying as the substitute for our sins. Romans 5:8 makes it clear: "But God demonstrates his own love for us in this: While we were still sinners, Christ died for us" (NIV). The key phrase here is "for us." Christ died *for*— in place of—*you* and *me*. The penalty of the cross was meant for us. Jesus substituted himself on our behalf, personally bearing the punishment and judgment for our sin. This is the biblical view of atonement.

Christus Victor is yet another theory of atonement that is prevalent in language of the New Testament. Christus Victor highlights Christ's victory over Satan, sin, and death on the cross and in his subsequent resurrection. Paul writes of Christ's victory over sin in Romans 6:23: "For the wages of sin is death, but the gift of God is eternal life in Christ Jesus our Lord" (NIV). One of my favorite verses declaring Christ's victory over death is 1 Corinthians 15:55,

"Where, O death, is your victory? Where, O death, is your sting?" (NIV). Numerous examples may be found in the New Testament clearly showing Christ as the Victor over the enemy, and the defeater of sin and death. But this victory is always accompanied by the work of Penal Substitution. Christ's victory is intricately tied to his dying on the cross in our place, paying the penalty of the offense of our sin to God (not paying off the Devil to let us go), and restoring our relationship with the Father.

Understanding the Reason Behind the Incarnation

It's vital to understand this aspect of the Son's incarnation. God the Father does not take sin lightly. He decreed that the penalty for sin is death, and someone must pay that penalty. Consider this: Let's say you have never sinned in your life; you've lived a perfect life. But me? Oh, how I have sinned—so much! But even with all of my sin, let's say you really love me a lot. So, we both go before God, and He rightly declares that I am a wretched sinner. But He clearly sees you are not. And just before God banishes me to ultimate death, you step up and say, "God, I will give my life to pay the penalty for Brad's sins." What does God say? God says, "Okay," which means you're toast and I'm free to live in bliss. Now, let's say you also like my brother, but he too is a sinner. You say to God, "I want to give my life for Brad's brother too." What does God say? God says, "Sorry, but you, a perfect finite human being can only pay for one other person's sins and no more. It's a one-for-one proposition." Do you see the problem? That is why God had to send His Son to become fully human, live a perfect life, and remain fully God. Truly, Jesus is the only perfect human who could ever pay the price for one or all of our sins. Precisely because He was and is fully God, He was and is infinite, and therefore could pay for *every person's sins* by dying for the sins of all people. Christ died once, for all!

"But Jesus did this once for all when he offered himself as the sacrifice for the people's sins" (Hebrews 7:27b NLT). I'll talk more of this in Chapter Five: Salvation. The most often-quoted verse in the Bible tells us this very clearly:

> "For God so loved the world that he gave his one and only Son, that whoever believes in him shall not perish but have eternal life" (John 3:16 NIV).

That verse says a lot about the Father and how much He loves you and me. And it says a ton about the Son's reason—or role—in being sent. He came to be the Savior of the world. Sometimes I hear well-meaning Christ-followers and even pastors pray, "Thank you Father for dying on the cross for our sins." That's nice, but it is woefully inaccurate, and it confuses the roles of the persons of the Trinity. That's not the role the Father played. That was the role of the Son. Thank the Father for sending the Son to die. Thank Jesus for the dying. If you come over to my house for dinner and my wife has labored all day to put a great meal on the table, don't thank me for making dinner, thank her. She did all the work. Just thank me for inviting you. I believe if we begin to understand and keep the roles of each person of the Holy Trinity clear, we will begin to get to know each person of the Trinity in a deeper way, which brings a lavish richness to our spiritual life.

One of the other roles God the Son took on when He became the man Jesus was that of a teacher who encouraged twelve men to follow Him and become His disciples. Eleven of them actually did. One betrayed Him. After Jesus died and rose again from the dead, this is what He told them:

> "All authority on Heaven and earth has been given to me. Therefore go and make disciples of all nations, baptizing them in the name of the Father, and of the Son and of the Holy Spirit" (Matthew 28:18 & 19 NIV).

Did you get that last part? Jesus clearly articulates the Father, the Son, and the Holy Spirit—what we call the Holy Trinity. He made no bones about it. Based on that verse alone, we can safely use the time-tested moniker of the Holy Trinity to describe the God of the universe. Jesus affirmed it, and there are numerous other Bible verses where the idea is clear.

The Reality of the Son

Some say Jesus is simply a myth on the same plane as Santa Claus or the Easter Bunny. Some say He was not a real historical figure. You must ask whether a myth could change how we measure time. Think of our dating system: BC and AD. Would a myth change and transform countless human lives for the better over thousands of years? The fact is, Jesus has had a greater impact than all the great leaders in human history put together! Even Albert Einstein recognized the authenticity of Jesus of Nazareth. Speaking of Jesus he said, "I am a Jew, but I am enthralled by the luminous figure of the Nazarene... No one can read the Gospels without feeling the actual presence of Jesus. His personality pulsates in every word. No myth is filled with such life."[12]

Remember Amir's scale?

A = Absolutely authentic.

B = Maybe authentic but questionable.

C = No way—pretty much all fabricated.

Jesus was and is an A all the way! He's the real deal and the ultimate superhero.

At the beginning of this section on the Son of God, I shared this verse: "In the beginning was the Word, and the Word was with God and the Word was God" (John 1:1 NIV). John uses the phrase *the Word* three times in this verse. In the ancient Greek, the language in which John wrote, *Word* is the Greek word *logos*. *Logos* is a fascinating word which described the seeking out of reason and meaning—the meaning of life. The word *logic* is derived from *logos*, and we use logic to arrive at meaning for all sorts of things. The *Word*, the *logos*, became flesh in order to bring true meaning to your life and mine. I would even go as far as to say you will never truly understand the meaning of your life until you meet Jesus.

If you want to meet Him for yourself and find true meaning in your life, ask Him personally. Sincerely say to Him in a humble prayer, "Jesus, forgive me, lead me and walk with me." Then watch what He does. If you embrace Jesus first as your Savior who forgives you of all your sins, who will rescue you from the muck of your life, your life will be transformed. Because, when you get Jesus, you also get the Holy Spirit.

God the Holy Spirit

The role of God the Holy Spirit cannot be overstated. If God the Father is the Designer and the Son is the Builder, the Holy Spirit is the Empowerer. It's like a construction project. The Father created the plans, the Son is the on-site project superintendent, and the Holy Spirit empowers the work. In the second sentence of the Bible, we are told the Holy Spirit hovered over the waters when the world was being created. The Holy Spirit empowered many Old Testament men and women to do remarkable things. When the Holy Spirit came on the day of Pentecost fifty days after Jesus' resurrection, believers, filled and empowered by the Holy Spirit, began to radically change the world. Jesus said, "But you will receive power when the Holy Spirit comes on you; and you will be my witnesses in Jerusalem, and in all Judea and Samaria, and to the ends of the earth" (Acts 1:8 NIV). Power! Power for what? To point people to Jesus. The Holy Spirit always points people to Jesus. That's His primary role in us.

The Holy Spirit is the giver of gifts as well. In his first letter to the church at Corinth, the Apostle Paul made that clear: *"There are different kinds of gifts, but the same Spirit distributes* them. There are different kinds of service, but the same Lord. There are different kinds of working, but in all of them and in everyone it is the same God at work" (1 Corinthians 12:4-6 NIV). So, the Holy Spirit gives the gifts, and the church is empowered to reach the world for Christ. But also take notice of these phrases within the verse above: *"the same Spirit, the same Lord, the same God."* We can easily see these as a reference to the Holy Trinity, where Spirit equals the Holy Spirit, Lord equals the Son, and God equals the Father. Or those words could simply be affirming the Holy Spirit is God, the third person of the Holy Trinity. Either way, it's clear the Holy Spirit is God.

The Holy Spirit is not an "it," but a person. This means He cares deeply for us and guides and directs us in all our ways. And just like we can pray to the Father and the Son, we can also pray to the Holy Spirit. In fact, have you ever been in such a state of confusion, depression, pain, or apathy that you knew you should pray, but just didn't know *what* to pray? I sure have. The following is a great verse to pray when those situations arise:

"Likewise the Spirit helps us in our weakness. For we do not know what to pray for as we ought, but the Spirit himself intercedes for us with groanings too deep for words" (Romans 8:26 ESV).

Did you catch that? The Spirit *himself.* That's a personal pronoun, meaning we can know the Holy Spirit as a person. We can have a personal relationship with the Holy Spirit. And when we don't know how to pray, we can cry out: "Holy Spirit, intercede for me with sighs or groanings too deep for words." I have done this on many occasions and the Holy Spirit always seems to lead me or comfort me, or both.

The Bible also calls us to be led by the Holy Spirit (Romans 8:14). For example, when my oldest son, Willie, was seventeen, he went through an extended period of darkness in his life. As a dad and a parent, it was so difficult. One morning I was on my knees, talking to God about it all. A thought came to me: "Let go and let God." It seemed so spiritual! *It had to be from God*, I thought. So, I prayed, "Lord, I'm letting go of my son and giving him to You. I'm done. I can't take it anymore." The Holy Spirit confronted in that moment: "No you don't!" And the Holy Spirit gave me one word, "Tenacious! Like never before, you tenaciously go after your son!" Wow! A few weeks later, I was scheduled to take Willie out to dinner just to talk and connect. It was November and getting cold at night in the Pacific Northwest. I texted him after school:

"When can I pick you up?"

"Later dad, I just need a little space right now."

"Okay."

A few hours go by. I text again: "Willie, let me pick you up and we'll go eat."

"Not yet."

Two hours later: "Willie, what's up?"

Text: "Dad, I'm not worthy to be called your son."

Whoa, tears! I text him back: "What? Where's all this coming from?"

And he goes dark. Off the grid! No response. I'm scared. Ann's scared. Our youngest son, Nathan, is very concerned and begins to pray. We pray and pray and pray, all the while calling friends and trying to text him and find out where he might be. Nothing.

We spoke with our daughter Sarah in Australia and she gets a prayer chain going with her college friends at school. About midnight, I fall asleep till about 2 AM. Still no Willie. I lay in my bed and start praying again. "Get up! Go look for him," is all I sense in my spirit—the Holy Spirit is speaking to me. (We learned later this was the exact time our daughter was lifting her brother up in worship and prayer Down Under.).

I started driving out of our little town toward the town his school was in, about eight miles. I cry out to God, "Lord, my son is lost, I'm lost, and I have no idea where to look. But Holy Spirit, you know, you know exactly where he is!" (Yes, I'm crying out audibly and specifically to the Holy Spirit!) The night was dark and cold as I drove along, looking in storefronts hoping I might see him. Nothing. "Turn right," I hear in my spirit. I was now driving toward the school. "Turn left," I hear. Then again, "Turn right." And I come upon an elementary school.

I drive toward the back and shine the lights of my car into a covered play area. Nothing there. I begin to back out and I hear in my spirit, "Get out!" I get out, turn my iPhone flashlight on and go around the corner and there, on the ground and curled up in a sleeping bag is my Willie. Tears! Joy! Relief! Awe! I tear up every time I tell that story because it is such a God story! God never gives up. The Holy Spirit did know exactly where Willie was. I had no clue. The Holy Spirit led me that night to miraculously find my son. There is simply no other explanation. It was like finding a needle in a very large haystack. There is no way that would have happened without being led by an all-knowing God! *That* is the person of the Holy Spirit.

Why would the Holy Spirit lead me to Willie? Love! The Holy Spirit gives us love, which will then grow within us until it is manifested and exemplified in our lives. The Bible calls this the Fruit of the Spirit, because like fruit, it will be seen blossoming, growing, maturing, evident to all who see it. As I stated in Chapter One, the whole Bible was written to help us increase in loving God and loving people. Jesus emphasizes the importance that our lives are characterized by love when he declares, "…everyone will know that you are my disciples, if you love one another" (John 13:35 NIV).

One of the greatest and most impactful evidences of the Holy Spirit's activity in our lives is the increase of the Fruit of the Spirit, which the Apostle Paul lists as: "Love, joy, peace, patience, kindness, goodness, faithfulness, gentleness, and self-control" (Galatians 5:22-23 NIV). One of the big buzzword topics of our time is "emotional intelligence." Look at that list of the nine Fruits of the Spirit. If you and I operated increasingly in all of those, we would be some of the most emotionally intelligent people on the planet. Now, look at that list again—then think of Jesus. He constantly operated in full capacity in all those Fruits of the Spirit. One of the great sayings among Christ-Followers is, "I just want to be more like Jesus." I love that! The Holy Spirit longs to produce His fruits increasingly in you and me so we can love our fellow brothers and sisters in Christ more, and so we will be more attractive to people who don't know Jesus yet.

We can also grieve the Holy Spirit! We do this when we claim to follow Jesus but act more like the Devil. One example of this is anger and rage. I see way too many self-proclaimed Christ-followers who are so angry and easily offended. I believe I have grieved the Holy Spirit in such a fashion over the years…

The year was 2014. Some people at our church got upset with me, their pastor. It happens. I tried to pacify them and work things out, but it wasn't to be. It was such an emotionally draining scenario. I was running on fumes. I voiced my feelings to my wife, and she was very understanding. But then I got angry at *her*. My anger hurt her, and I believe it grieved the Holy Spirit. I wish I could say it was simply that one situation, but over the years it was a reoccurring theme in my life. I finally had to come to terms with it. I did get some counseling, but more than that, I went to the Ultimate Counselor—the Holy Spirit. I got on my knees and asked Him specifically for the Fruit of the Spirit of self-control. Guess what? He gave it to me, and I rarely get angry like that anymore. But when I come close, I always, immediately ask for forgiveness.

Which Fruit of the Spirit do you need to increase in your life? Ask Him today! There are other roles the Holy Spirit plays. He draws us to salvation. He makes us holy. These are subjects I will cover in Chapter Five.

Final thoughts on the Holy Trinity

Get to know the Holy Trinity. Build a relationship with each divine person of the Holy Trinity.

Learn and appreciate their roles on a deeper level. Walk with Jesus. Cry out to God, "Abba Father," as Jesus did. Be led by the Spirit and pray in the Spirit.

In 1987, I went to a singles retreat where our Presbyterian church singles department invited a Catholic monk, Father Francis, as the keynote speaker. I thought it was a bit odd, but then I thought, "Well, he must be single!" It was during the end of a session as he prayed that I first began to understand the personal nature of the Holy Trinity. Father Francis ended his prayer by saying something like this: "Father, thank you for being such a great and awesome God; Jesus, thank you for saving us; and Holy Spirit, guide us as we seek to do your will." Bingo! That was a huge "AHA!" moment for me. It's like I was suddenly and very personally introduced to each member of the Godhead who authentic Christ-followers call the Holy Trinity, and I've been praying in a similar way ever since.

I hope this chapter helps you see the value of seeking and understanding the nature of each person of the Holy Trinity. When you do, your relationship with God will be so much deeper!

Jesus said, "But when he, the Spirit of truth, comes, he will guide you into all truth…" (John 16:13a NIV). The Holy Spirit will lead you and me into all truth! I love that! The truth is, we need the Holy Spirit to lead us in all truth because there is a ton of deception out there. We'll see that in the next chapter.

How should we score the Holy Trinity on Amir's scale?

A = Absolutely authentic.

B = Maybe authentic but questionable.

C = No way—pretty much all fabricated.

There is so much more that could be said about the Holy Trinity and where each person of the Trinity shows up in the Bible. But I'm convinced the Holy Trinity is an "A" on Amir's scale, as it should be on the scale of every person who calls themselves a Christ-follower.

three

The Devil

When my son Willie was a young boy, he used to sleepwalk. It was an odd thing my wife and I did not really understand. We made inquiries into psychologists and medical doctors, but no one gave us anything definitive other than to be very careful not to wake him up while he was sleepwalking—just guide him toward his bed and do your best to get him back, fully asleep, without waking him. Normally the process would take about an hour. This went on sporadically for a few years.

When Willie was eight years old, I went to a men's conference with a group of men to the Colorado Rockies. The retreat leader spoke about how many Christ-followers have ceased to believe the Devil and his demons are real. He encouraged us to not be wooed to sleep by the Devil. He strongly directed us to become spiritual warriors for our wives and families. When I returned home to Oregon late one night, Willie was fast asleep in *my* bed next to his mother. I was dead tired from the journey home, so I carefully picked Willie up so as not to wake him, took him over to his bedroom, and gently put him down in his bed.

Suddenly, Willie sits up, "Dad, Dad, Dad, they're after me, Dad!" He was asleep, and I lamented, "Oh no, I am so tired, I do not want to deal with this for the next hour." Then I thought, "I wonder if he's being oppressed by a demon." So, I put my arms around him, and said out loud, "In the name of Jesus, I command you demon to flee from my son! Now!" And then I said it one more time, louder for good measure. Within one second, I was able to softly put Willie's head back down on his pillow, and he fell fast asleep. "Wow," I thought. But that's not the end of the story.

The next morning, at about 7 AM, Willie comes dancing into my bedroom and says, "Hey Dad! I missed you, Dad! Man, I feel good this morning! I haven't felt this good in a long time." I hold back tears as I recall the moment. I thought, "Of course you feel good Willie. You don't have a demon on your back oppressing your anymore." From that point forward, to this day, some nineteen years later, he has never had another sleepwalking episode. Yeah…I believe.

In the Bible story of Jesus casting out the demon in the son of a tired father, it says, "…He rebuked the impure spirit. 'You deaf and mute spirit' he said, 'I command you come out of him and never enter him again'" (Mark 9:25b NIV). I call that a battle prayer! That's very similar to what I did with Willie, but I invoked the name of Jesus. I always say, "In the strong name of Jesus," because I'm convinced the Devil and his cronies know exactly who Jesus is.

Make no mistake, the Devil and his demons are real, and the Devil is as deceptive as they come! I know…now you think I'm nuts.

Am I? Let's go there for a minute. Think about this: what if you had an enemy who was wreaking havoc all around you, getting you to be offended and angry at people you loved? What if that same enemy could get you to actively fight against friends, neighbors, relatives, and even your very own children and spouse? What if you began to see people being divided like never before? And, what if that divider could get you to believe he didn't exist? What if he could make you think your problem and my problem were strictly psychological? Brilliant, don't you think? That's the Devil! Satan and Lucifer are just a couple of his names. He exists in the spiritual realm and has legions of demons at his disposal to steal, kill, and destroy the love and relationships in your life and mine. Those are really the only things the Devil cares to do. Jesus said in John 10:10a, "The thief comes only to steal and kill and destroy" (NIV). Just look around our world. Seems like he's doing a pretty good job of it.

Jesus called the Devil, "the thief." The Devil is the ultimate thief—a *scammer*. Scammers try to steal money from people by making them believe they are getting some kind of benefit in return. On any given day, my email inbox is hit by any number of communications that are obvious scams. Some though, are not so obvious...

Many years ago, my wife and I bought a timeshare in Mexico. Recently I received a call from Fred (not his real name), an agent for a real-estate firm representing an investment group wanting to purchase the building our time-share was in. He said with the interest that had accrued over the last ten years, our share of the building was worth over $19,000. It sounded reasonable, and I told him to email me an offer, which I printed out and showed to my wife. She said, "Brad, it's scam." I said, "Honey, I think this guy is legit." She dismissed it, so I involved my assistant, Natalie, who has some experience with this sort of thing. She did a background check on Fred and found he was indeed a scammer who had bilked thousands of dollars from unsuspecting people. One day while I was sitting working on a Sunday message, Fred called to check up on the deal. I said, "Fred, bro, we did a background check on you. You are a total scammer and have ripped people off for thousands of dollars! Listen Fred, I'm a pastor, and know this: if you don't repent and turn to Jesus, you'll end up in Hell." Now, I wish I could report to you that Fred, with a contrite spirit, repented right there and then, confessed his sins, and put his faith in Jesus. Nope. Click! Fred hung up on me.

The Devil is a scammer, and he is scamming whole generations with his lies. One of his most popular con games right now is a major cultural deception involving love and freedom and sexuality. Think about it—the Devil hates the light and anything that is reflection of God. Humans are made in God's image and likeness. He made us male and female, he made us for the marriage relationship, and he made us for love and affection and procreation. Our sexuality is a key element of how God designed human beings to reflect His image. So, the Devil goes after our sexuality, and these days he has confused it like never before. It's all his major scam on humanity, and people are falling for it. What's the price? Not $19,000…but your very soul.

The irony is many Americans don't believe in the Devil. Surveys vary, but a YouGov survey found only 57 percent of Americans believe the Devil exists. The survey did say around 80 percent of Christians believe the Devil is real, but just 25 percent of Muslims and only 17 percent of Jews believe in his existence.[13] Another survey stated that only 17 percent of US Catholics believe the Devil is a real being, while 83 percent believe Satan is merely a symbol.[14] These are very troubling numbers. Jewish people especially should believe the Devil is real after they endured the most wretched evil our modern world has ever seen during the World War Two holocaust perpetrated by Nazi Germany. But they don't. How can that be? Deception!

Where do we find the truth about the Devil? From Jesus! Jesus believed in the existence and activity of the Devil, demons, and the evil realm. He knew it was all too real. The gospels are full of true stories of Jesus encountering demons and casting them out of people. In a telling encounter, a man who had a demon-possessed son asked Jesus, "If you can do anything, take pity on us and help us." Jesus said "If you can? Everything is possible for one who believes" (Mark 9:22-23 NIV). Often, when this Scripture is preached, the emphasis is rightly placed on believing in Jesus. However, part of the belief that both father and Jesus' disciples were missing was the belief in the existence of demons and the demonic realm. In perhaps the most humble, honest admission of doubt, the desperate father exclaimed, "I do believe; help me overcome my unbelief" (Mark 9:24 NIV). And Jesus rebuked the evil spirit. It left the boy, and the boy was restored. There is much more to the story, like Jesus stating a lack of prayer was the reason His disciples couldn't cast this demon out. Belief and prayer. Perhaps a vibrant prayer life would help us enter into the reality of the spiritual realm and could help us see more of what was so clear to Jesus, even the dark stuff. Then, perhaps, we would believe so much more!

Who is the Devil and where did Satan and his demonic followers come from? Let's take a look.

The Devil in the Old Testament

There are several Bible passages that allude to Satan's, or Lucifer's, pre-sin existence and the reason for his excommunication from Heaven. Key scriptures are found in Isaiah 14, Ezekiel 28, and the Book of Job. You can read them for yourself, but I will highlight this passage from Isaiah chapter 14:

"How you are fallen from heaven,
O shining star, son of the morning!
You have been thrown down to the earth,
you who destroyed the nations of the world.
For you said to yourself,
"I will ascend to heaven and set my throne above
God's stars.
I will preside on the mountain of the gods
far away in the north.
I will climb to the highest heavens
and be like the Most High."
Instead, you will be brought down to the place
of the dead,
down to its lowest depths" (Isaiah 14:12-15 NLT).

Here's my understanding of what is happening here in Isaiah 14. In this passage, Isaiah is actually writing about the empire nation of Babylon. God had called upon and inspired Babylon to teach the Israelites a lesson for their sinfulness. But wicked Babylon would go too far. And, while much of Isaiah the prophet's focus is on Babylon in these verses, it appears God switches Isaiah's focus to the *source* of Babylon's evil—the Devil. And here we get a rare glimpse of the Devil's journey from Heaven to Earth, from being a brilliant angelic being to an arrogant tyrant, so consumed with himself that he wants God to bow down before him.

God created Lucifer as the most powerful and splendid of all the angels in Heaven. Understand this: Lucifer and all the angels are *created* beings. All the beings, animals, planets, stars, etc., were created by God, who has existed eternally, before there was even time to measure his existence. Lucifer had a created beginning. God is infinite. Lucifer is finite. At some point before God created humanity, He created Lucifer. But Lucifer got jealous of God and didn't want to serve Him. Lucifer wanted God's job and to have everyone bow to him. It kind of sounds like a Marvel superhero movie. I'm thinking of Loki—Thor's misguided brother. So, Lucifer began to recruit other angels to serve him and rebel against God, and God threw him, along with all his "converts," out of Heaven down to earth. It was at that point that Lucifer became Satan, the totally wicked Devil, and all the angels that followed him became demons. According to Revelation chapter 12, one-third of all the angels in Heaven were tossed out and have since roamed the earth in another dimension called the spiritual realm, wreaking havoc. Let me reiterate, the Devil and the demons are created, formerly angelic beings. Verse 15 in Isaiah chapter 14 above is telling. While Lucifer's plans were grand, the key word is "Instead!" Instead, you will be brought down! Where? To the place of the dead! To the pit of hell!

Now, let's pause for a moment. This last paragraph needs to be honestly graded. The truth is, we don't have all the information about Satan's pre-fall existence. Many Bible scholars would likely agree with how I interpreted it. Some would call some things into question. Like the word *Lucifer* for example. Originally, in Hebrew, it was *Morning Star*. When it was translated into Latin, it was *Lucifer*. So, Lucifer is really a Latin word that never was translated correctly into English. But again, I believe what I've written is fairly accurate.

That said, just on the above paragraph let's look again at Amir's grading scale:

A = Absolutely authentic.
B = Maybe authentic but questionable.
C = No way—pretty much all fabricated.

I'd say let's give that paragraph a B, maybe a B plus, on the grounds that it requires some extra interpretation.

The Devil in the New Testament

Jesus and the writers of the New Testament had much to say about the Devil. In one instance, Jesus sent seventy-two of His early followers to several villages, and when they came back we're told: "The seventy-two returned with joy and said, 'Lord, even the demons submit to us *in your name*.' He replied, 'I saw Satan fall like lightning from Heaven'" (Luke 10:17-18 NIV, italics added).

The demons submitted to the seventy-two when they used the name of Jesus. That's pretty cool. But look at verse 18 again: Jesus says, "I saw Satan fall like lightning from Heaven." Whoa! But how did Jesus see what happened so long before? To understand this, we must go back to the Trinity. Remember, before Jesus became a man, he was the eternal Son of God, who we call the "pre-incarnate

Son." Incarnate means to be *embodied in flesh*. Before the Son took on flesh and became the man Jesus, He existed in Heaven as God the Son. So, Lucifer and all the angels knew who He was. In fact, the Son created them: "Through him all things were made. Without him nothing was made that has been made" (John 1:3 NIV). It is even more interesting as we read in the Gospel of Mark where a demon-possessed man said to Jesus, "What do you want with me, Jesus, Son of the Most High God?" (Mark 5:7 NIV) Why would the demon know who Jesus was? Because that demon, and all demons, knew from their pre-fallen state who the Son of God was. They knew who he was then, they knew who he was is the New Testament stories, and they know who he is now! As strange as it may seem, Jesus is actually their creator.

Why would Jesus create demons? The answer is: He didn't! He created angels who had free will to love and obey God—or not. The Devil and his legions chose not to obey God, so He threw those disobedient angelic beings out of Heaven, and from that point they became desperately wicked demons who have absolutely no ability to do good.

Why did God throw them out of Heaven? Because Heaven is a holy place. Only holiness resides there, so the wicked angels could not. We will discuss more on holiness in a few more chapters.

Possession versus Oppression

We read about Jesus and his disciples casting out demons, and it brings up the question of just who can be possessed. As we consider the subject of salvation in Chapter Five, we will see that once a person puts their faith in Christ, the Holy Spirit enters their soul. This also means that once the Holy Spirit is in you, a demon cannot possess you. I like to say it like this: once a person puts their faith in Christ they can no longer be *possessed,* but they can be *oppressed.* That is my understanding of Scripture, which may fall into the realm of secondary doctrines. I believe Willie was being oppressed, not possessed. He had a demonic spirit bothering him from the outside, but not possessing him inside. Make sense?

It's pretty clear that demons are oppressing Christians all over the planet. The book of Revelation reveals that the Devil is full of rage and on a rampage! Revelation chapter 12 covers a large part of the spiritual timeline, beginning when Lucifer rebelled and was thrown out of Heaven with his rebellious angels, through to their activity against Christians even to our current day. Satan is described in this chapter as the dragon. Let's look at Revelation 12:17: "Then the dragon was enraged at the woman and went off to wage war against the rest of her offspring—those who keep God's commands and hold fast their testimony about Jesus" (Revelation 12:17 NIV).

The "woman" in this verse could be Jesus' earthly mother Mary, or, she could be the Church, which is described as the Bride of Christ. We can't know for sure. What we can know are two things:

1) Satan is enraged.

2) He's waging war against anyone who is faithfully following God's word and proclaims Jesus as their Lord and Savior.

We are at war! Whether you want to be or not, if you claim to be a faithful Christ-follower, if Jesus is your Savior, Lord, and King, you will be oppressed and attacked. It's not a matter of if. It's just a matter of when and how. That means we need to be ready. The Apostle Paul tells us how to be ready in his letter to the church at Ephesus:

> "Finally, be strong in the Lord and his mighty power. Put on the full armor of God, so that you can take your stand against the devil's schemes for our struggle is not against flesh and blood, but against the rulers, against the authorities, against the power of this dark world and again the spiritual forces of evil in the Heavenly realms" (Ephesians 6:10-12 NIV).

The battle is not against your neighbor, friend, business associate, classmate, or relative. It's against Satan and his demons. Paul goes on to say, "Therefore put on the full armor of God..." (Ephesians 6:13a NIV). One of my greatest concerns is that I have come to believe beyond a shadow of a doubt that a spiritual war is going on all around us, a spiritual war that would make the battles in the *Lord of the Rings* trilogy look like child's play. Think about that for just a moment. A huge spiritual war is raging all around us, yet many Christ-followers daily walk out onto the battlefield virtually naked. Paul tells us to armor up. Every day! He says, and this is my paraphrase: 1) Get daily doses of God's truth through His Word, the Bible. 2) Pray. 3) Live a right and good life. 4) Make sure you know Jesus and the gospel of grace and never forget it. 5) Trust God always.

How worn is your armor? Do you put it on every day? Remember you were made in the image and likeness of God—

Imago Dei! Know that the Devil longs to destroy the image of God *in* you and *on* you. The most effective way for him to do that is to tempt you to sin. Any kind of sin will do. He will not only tempt you to sin, but make you believe you are not really sinning at all. That is how he thinks he will win the battle between good and evil, by tempting you and deceiving you.

I really love books and movies that portray the classic battles of good versus evil. I'm convinced those movies are made because even in the hearts and minds of many unbelieving Hollywood producers and screenwriters, they know good and evil exist. They just don't realize that what they are writing and filming—the basic truth of good versus evil—God Himself put in their hearts. Christ-followers should knowingly practice good and be armored up and be ready for evil every day.

Have you noticed lately we are increasingly offended by each other? The best trick the media uses to get a following is to goad us into being offended. Politically, the left is offended by the right, and the right is offended by the left. One wrong word and we don't forgive, we condemn. The truth is, Satan loves us to be offended by each other. Author and speaker John Bevere wrote a book called *The Bait of Satan*. I encourage every Christ-follower to read it and apply it. We did a whole sermon series one year called *Unoffendable*, based on the Bible with help from Brant Hansen's book *Unoffendable*. You can watch or listen to the series online at www.epichouse.church.

Understanding how *not* to be easily offended saves marriages, businesses, churches, and many friendships, and it will bring so much joy into your life. Every time we get offended, we get hooked by the bait of Satan and he uses it to steal, kill, and destroy relationships and rob our joy. We just saw in Revelation chapter 12 that Satan is enraged. That's really, really angry!

Peter, one of Jesus' closest disciples, wrote: "Be alert and of sober mind. Your enemy the devil prowls around like a roaring lion looking for someone to devour" (1 Peter 5:8 NIV). A roaring lion! Sounds enraged to me! Have you ever been around a rageaholic or someone who is just angry, bitter, and resentful all the time? Would you describe them as emotionally mature or emotionally immature? Emotionally immature for sure!

God's word says, "Do not let the sun go down while you're still angry, and do not give the devil a foothold" (Ephesians 4:26b NIV). God says get rid of your anger quickly. The world says to nurture it, that it's justified! I've been sober, one hundred percent free from alcohol, for over thirty-five years now, only by the grace of God. I learned in Alcoholics Anonymous early on in my sobriety, "Bitterness and resentment are simply anger with mold on it." If you want to be a miserable person, hold onto anger, learn not to forgive—be bitter, be resentful. Give the Devil a big foothold in your life. He loves it. Be angry and offended and miserable! Satan sure is! He's been enraged for thousands of years. He sure must be ugly! It reminds me of Emperor Palpatine, Darth Vader's master in Star Wars. Pretty ugly! There is another way.

Peter Scazzero, in his great book *The Emotionally Healthy Church*, writes: "It is not possible to be spiritually mature while remaining emotionally immature."[15] They go hand in hand. I say, "The most spiritually mature person in the room is the person least likely to be offended, even when they should be." I'm convinced the more spiritually and emotionally immature and the angrier you are, the more likely you will be used as a pawn of the Devil.

The Devil is always looking for any opportunity to take Christ-followers out of the game. He tried it with Jesus, and he will try it again and again with us.

A few years ago, a group from our church went to visit Wayne Cordeiro at New Hope Church in Oahu, Hawaii. (I know, it's a dirty job but someone had to do it.) One day, Wayne took us to a passage in Daniel where it shows some of the Devil's strategies:

> "He will speak against the Most High and *oppress* his holy people and try to change the set times and the laws. The holy people will be delivered into his hands for a time, times, and half a time" (Daniel 7:25 NIV, *italics added*).

Wayne shared that the word *oppress* in this verse is an ancient word having to do with coinage, which means to *wear down*. In these ancient times, often when coinage would lose its luster and the images and markings on the coin would be worn down, the coin would be worth less than the face value of the coin. Personally, I've seen this in my own travels to Africa. The exchange rate for US $100 bills is higher for brand new crisp bills. Worn, older bills are worth less. Satan does that with us. He goes after us and causes havoc in our relationships. He tries to make us feel emotionally drained to the point of feeling worthless, or literally, *worth less*. Have you ever felt it? Know this, and this is my interpretation, that *time, times, and half a time,* means Satan will be relentless in trying to wear us down! How do we battle that? Wayne said, "Be re-minted into God's image daily by spending time in God's word and prayer." That is what the Apostle Paul referred to as armoring up!

A few final thoughts about the Devil. The Devil has been around for thousands of years. That means he's a mastermind of deception. The Bible's word for Devil is *diabolos.* We get the word *diabolical* from that word. The Devil is diabolical, and there is no good in him. NONE. Don't ever be a Devil sympathizer. He's incredibly deceptive. He'll present things that look very attractive. He did it to Jesus. The Devil even used God's word to try to get a lie past Jesus. You can read it for yourself in Luke chapter 4 when Satan tempted Jesus. The Bible says, "For Satan himself masquerades as an angel of light" (2 Corinthians 11:14 NIV). These days, Satan is doing an amazing job convincing many people that evil is good and good is evil, that light is darkness and darkness is light. He's been doing it for many centuries.

Have you seen the COEXIST Bumper Sticker?[16]

I really can live with people of other faiths. I can and do love them and even eat with them and enjoy our time together. That said, I hope to show you in a few chapters why I chose Christianity over other faith systems. But perhaps you have seen that blue and white Coexist bumper sticker prominently displayed on the back of the car in front of you, its letters created out of a variety of religious and cultural iconography. While the sentiment appears on the surface to be a good thing, the message is ultimately stating: "Hey, these different beliefs and ideologies are all good, equal, and true." But are they? The dot on the "i" is the witchcraft pentagram symbol, which many Satanists use to worship Satan.

Also problematic is the "S," which uses the symbol for Taoism, where we get the Yin and the Yang. It's a cool logo, which I've seen many Christians wear on a chain or even have it tattooed on their body. But most often they don't know what it truly means, that, in essence, good and evil are equal, and they both need to be equal to keep the balance in the universe. But this isn't reality. Why does good always win in good-versus-evil movies and literature? Because we intrinsically know good is *greater* than evil. God is good! Very good. *Perfectly* good. And God is so much greater than any evil. It's not even close. To wear that logo as a Christ-follower is to promote a significant deception. I could get into several other issues here, but I'd just encourage you to look up and understand all the symbols of each religion and ideology represented before you invest in or display those symbols. The early Christians didn't have cars to put bumper stickers on, but they had wagons. Perhaps on some of them was the word Syncretism—it's similar to Coexist. It would be like putting all the religions in one big spiritual stew pot. Some like that idea, but I warn against it. Love those of different religions but be careful of getting thrown in the Devil's stewpot of Syncretism. It's just one of the Devil's schemes to derail your faith in Jesus.

Remember, as stated above, the New Testament word for the Devil is *diabolos*. It means, slanderer, cunning, adversary. It is aligned with pure evil. There is no good in him! The Devil follows no rules other than his agenda to steal, kill, and destroy (John 10:10). The Geneva Convention refers to how dignified countries should conduct themselves when at war with each other. They convened and made up rules for how they should treat women and children and prisoners. It has provided some honorable guidelines even when two or more countries are engaged in the brutality of war against each other. But like the wickedness of terrorism, with the Devil, there are no rules! He will go after you, your kids, your spouse—whomever. The Devil is the ultimate terrorist. No Rules! If Jesus is the ultimate superhero, the Devil is the ultimate villain.

So, be careful. While I don't see the Devil around every corner, I do see him wreaking havoc with people everywhere, even children. I strongly advise you not to play with things that are aligned with the evil realm. Don't invite the Devil into your home or life via Ouija boards or palm readers or psychics. God says all that kind of stuff is of the Devil (see Deuteronomy 18:9-12).

When someone consistently attacks with a voice of blame and shame, know that the person who is blaming and shaming may well be influenced by the Devil or one of his demons. God is not a voice of blame and shame. While He does convict us of our sin, and at times allows us to feel shame so we will repent and turn back to Him, his goal is always grace and restoration.

Now you know that the Devil is real, and we are at war. But Jesus defeated the Devil at the cross and won the victory at His resurrection. For a time, before Jesus returns, the Devil and his cronies are still roaming the earth looking for followers and especially looking for followers of Jesus to neutralize, which he often does by tempting us to sin.

In the next chapter, we'll take a close look at the struggle if sin. Before we do, answer the following:

How real is the Devil on Amir's scale?

A = Absolutely authentic.

B = Maybe authentic but questionable.

C = No way—pretty much all fabricated.

I'll let you put your answer in right here: A, B or C? _____

four

Sin

Recently, I was making breakfast and an egg fell off the counter and made a mess all over the floor. "Gravity," I thought. If that egg would have rolled off the counter and just floated in the air, it would make my life so much easier. Admittedly, the benefits of gravity probably outweigh the messes it causes. But let's be clear: the messes in our lives made by *gravity* are nothing compared to the messes caused by *depravity*.

Sin. Life is a struggle, and sin is the culprit.

I often ask people, "Have you ever sinned?" The response I get most is, "Oh, yeah!" Everyone seems to know what sin is, even atheists. Honestly, I believe most atheists would agree with the first four words of the following Bible verse: "For all have sinned and fall short of the Glory of God" (Romans 3:23 NIV). But where did sin come from? What is sin? How do you define it?

The English word "sin" comes from an ancient archery term. It means "to miss the mark." And it makes sense when we look at sin as "failing to hit the intended target." The problem with that analogy is, we might get the idea that with enough training we can shoot straight, and everything will be fine! Not true.

Jesus stated the problem clearly, "This is the verdict: Light has come into the world, but people loved darkness instead of light because their deeds were evil. Everyone who does evil hates the light, and will not come into the light for fear that their deeds will be exposed" (John 3:19-20 NIV). How can you shoot straight in the darkness without light? Humans love darkness, and that love of darkness draws us into sin, which compels us all the more to remain in the darkness rather than choose the light.

We sin because we suffer from the terminal disease of Sin (with a capital "S"). We sin because humanity was infected with the Sin disease way back in the Garden of Eden when Satan coaxed Eve and Adam to eat the forbidden fruit. One bite ruined humankind! Everything got so messed up that we not only missed the mark, but we also began to shoot in the wrong direction—even at God himself! It got so bad that God chose to destroy the whole planet in a flood and start over. Ultimately, sin is human self-centeredness.

Sin is our most basic problem. Many would even say that sin is what makes us human. To fix it, some say we need more education. Some say we need more money. Some say we need more social sensitivity and awareness. All of these are fine options toward improving the level of ignorance about the effects of sin, but they miss the mark on eliminating the root cause of sin.

Sin has wide-reaching effects. In 2017, three Category 4 hurricanes hit the US and its territories—Harvey, Irma, and Maria.

That was very unusual. It's the first time it has happened since they started keeping records in 1851.[17] Now consider how many people were killed by these "acts of God." While the final count could be adjusted, it was approximately 196 people. Tragic? Absolutely. Then compare this to how many people have been murdered in the US by other people. In 2016 alone the number is 17,250.[18] That's just the United States. How can this be?

The answer is Sin! "You shall not murder" is listed at number six in the Ten Commandments. Adultery is another tragic sin. I couldn't find a definitive number, but people who track these statistics say as many as one-third of all marriages are impacted by infidelity. Let's do a little easy math. According to statista.com,[19] there are about 60 million couples in the United States. That means about 20 million couples are impacted by adultery. As I process that stratospheric number, I'm amazed the murder rate isn't higher as a result—if you know what I mean. Twenty million couples with one or the other or both engaging in adultery! It's astounding. Just think how that one sin impacts not just those couples, but their children as well. It's hard to fathom. Suffice it to say, sin is responsible for the super-majority of human problems.

How did sin get here? It started with the first human beings. God told Adam and Eve they could have everything—anything!—except *one* thing. He said not to touch or eat from the tree in the middle of the garden. He gave them a command not to do one simple thing. Could they resist? With the urging of the Devil, evidently not. They disobeyed God, gave in to the Devil, and committed the first human sin—and the rest is history. Sin infected the entire human spiritual gene pool, which in turn infected everything else. It has been said that we commit sins because we are infected with sin. All our problems, and all the world's problems, can be traced back to sin. It is the primary human disease. Sin takes away life, both physically and spiritually. Sin separates us from the God of all life. It puts up a wall between God and us, and us and others. Sin kills love!

Sin is messy and deceptive. Often when a person is stuck or trapped in sin, it is the very sin itself that a person is committing which tells the sinner, "You're okay," or "It's the other person's fault." Let me give you a personal example: I became an alcoholic sometime during my teen years. I drank and used drugs for a significant period of time—from twelve years old to twenty-eight years old. Many times after I got off work, I'd grab a 12-pack of Budweiser beer and within about three hours they'd all be gone. I'd down them all. I'd get up, go to work the next day, be on time, work hard, and do it all over again. Did I have a problem? *Nah! Work hard, play hard, baby!* That was my motto! I wasn't hurting anyone. I wouldn't drive—*most* of the time. What's the big deal anyway? Well, God calls drunkenness a sin—not just a sin, but debauchery. Really? Really!

Ironically, some of my partying friends intimated to me that I might have a problem with alcohol. They weren't Christians. They were pagan to the core, but they saw it. Why couldn't I see it? Worse, why would I get angry at them and deny it altogether? One word: pride. I was too proud to humble myself and admit I had a problem. Pride is what got Satan thrown out of Heaven. Pride is the mother of all sin and sins. Calling it "The Great Sin," C.S. Lewis stated, "The essential vice, the utmost evil, is pride. Unchastity, anger, greed, drunkenness, and all that, are mere flea-bites in comparison: it was through pride that the devil became the devil: pride leads to every other vice: it is the complete anti-God state of mind."[20]

As I extracted that amazing quote from C.S. Lewis' classic book *Mere Christianity*, I thought, "Man, I wish I would have written that." Some people steeped in pride may try to pass it off as their own. That's the sin of plagiarism, often driven by pride. Another word for pride I learned in AA years ago is EGO—Edge God Out. When I swear at a car that just cut me off, my ego justifies my action and tells me, "You're okay. The other driver is the problem." My ego is always pointing to others who are the problem and not myself. After all, *I'm okay*. I'm learning that when I need to justify my harsh actions, that's a big red flag that should tell me I'm *not* okay. I need help and I need God.

God is willing to give us all sorts of help. The fact is He has given us moral guidelines for living with Him and with each other. He gave them to us through His servant Moses around 3400 years ago. They are called the Ten Commandments. The Ten Commandments are kind of like moral guardrails, they prevent us from falling off the edge and tell us when we have fallen. Both are essential for a healthy community. Let's reflect at a few of them.

Consider adultery again. Most people would say it is wrong. Most people would say lying is wrong. Most people would say murder is wrong and stealing is wrong. Especially when it has to do with *other* people. But most people could probably define when any of these would be okay to engage in. We often try to figure out how to justify our sin. We try to reason away why in this situation it is just different. Or why in that situation, it can't really be called sin at all.

We even try to justify our sin to God, or explain it away as not our fault. But it's not new. In the book of Job, a book in the Old Testament many scholars believe to be the oldest book in the Bible, and perhaps the world's oldest book, God says this to Job, "Would you discredit my justice? Would you condemn me to justify yourself?" (Job 40:8 NIV). That's what we often do. We condemn or discredit God and His word to justify our sinful actions.

There is a disturbing trend in our world regarding sin. Many are deciding they don't want to struggle with it, so they deny it's even sin altogether, calling it "normal" and even embracing it. *Struggle.* It seems like a bad word, but I love that word. It shows me that sin has strength, but we can still fight against it. The writer of Hebrews knew something about struggling with sin. He writes, "In your struggle against sin, you have not resisted to the point of shedding your blood" (Hebrews 12:4 NIV). The verse clearly shows we will struggle with sin, but Jesus shed His blood to end our struggle. Keep that word in mind—*struggle.*

The Bible tells us in many places what various specific human sins are. In two verses, written to the church at Corinth, the Apostle Paul gives us a pretty good list of different types of sinners. See if you can identify with any:

"Or do you not know that wrongdoers will not inherit the kingdom of God? Do not be deceived: Neither the sexually immoral nor idolaters nor adulterers nor male prostitutes nor practicing homosexuals nor thieves nor the greedy nor drunkards nor slanderers nor swindlers will inherit the kingdom of God" (1 Corinthians 6:9-10 NIV).

God says if we, as sinners, choose to persist in these sins and never ask Him for forgiveness of these sins, we are in danger of not making it to Heaven, which means we will not inherit eternal life with Him in paradise. That's the truth. And that's scary. I count ten clear lifestyles of sin in these verses. Here's the truth about me: I have struggled with eight of these ten at different times in my life. ME…eight out of ten! I'm done for, right? Hold on.

The key word is *struggle*. Do we really struggle with sin? My great concern is that we have a culture in America that says, "You don't have to struggle with your sin anymore. In fact, damn you if you even call it a sin. It is to be celebrated. We need to be proud of it!" they say. Back in my drinking days, oh how I celebrated my drunken stupors. My buddies and I would laugh and tell our drunk-a-logues, complete with sexual exploits, proudly. But, according to God and His word, it was, is, and always will be sin. Here's an ancient truth worth remembering: "If we claim to be without sin we deceive ourselves and the truth is not in us" (1 John 1:8 NIV).

Remember what God asked Job: "Would you condemn me to justify yourself?" We actually condemn what God's Word says about sin in order to justify ourselves. Here is the scary part: When we decide what God has called sin is no longer sinful, we come dangerously close to committing the unforgivable sin, which Jesus said is blasphemy against the Holy Spirit (Mark 3:29). Think about it this way: As I stated in the first chapter of this book, the Holy Spirit supernaturally breathed the words of the Bible into forty-plus human authors. The Bible itself, breathed by the Holy Spirit says, "The grass withers and the flowers fall, but the word of the Lord stands forever" (1 Peter 1:24a-25 NIV). Jesus said, "Heaven and earth will pass away, but my words will never pass away" (Luke 21:33 NIV). Can we just take scissors to God's Word and cut out what we don't like in order to feel good about ourselves? God has clearly called sin in His unchanging word, the Bible. When we say, "It's not sin," we are disagreeing with the Holy Spirit, and come close to blaspheming against the Holy Spirit. Merriam-Webster defines blasphemy as "The act of insulting or showing contempt or lack of reverence for God."

A few years ago, some of our church leaders again spent some time with Wayne Cordeiro, and this was the topic of discussion. Wayne asked the question, "What sin is unforgivable?" We responded, "Blasphemy against the Holy Spirit." Then Wayne asked, "How do you define it?" To which he answered, "It's the one sin we refuse to turn from or repent of." Wow! Ponder that!

I have often heard, and even said myself, "If you are worried about committing the sin of blasphemy against the Holy Spirit, you haven't. Because if you have, you wouldn't be worried about it." It means that if you still care about the truth of what the Spirit says about sin, then you haven't shown total contempt for what He has to say. I like that. However, it may be too simple an answer. Remember the Devil? He is incredibly diabolical and clever. What if he could get you and me, and people we know and love, to disagree with God on what constitutes a sin? What if he increasingly desensitized our spirit to the problem of our sin? What if he could prey on our pride so much that we would get angry at people saying what we are doing is sinful? What if he could twist it in our minds so much that we sought allies to rally around us to support our sin? What if we became so proud of our sins that we stopped calling them sins at all, and therefore never turned from them? What if we committed blasphemy against the Holy Spirit without any thought or remorse or worry? I believe that's what we are potentially seeing everywhere in our culture these days, and it must really grieve the heart of God.

When God is grieved by our sin, we should feel it. I grew up with five brothers and one sister. During my elementary and middle school years, my closest brother was Boyd. He was thirteen months older than me. Somewhere in our high school years, I suspected he engaged in homosexuality. In subsequent years he outwardly lived a gay lifestyle, and I hated him for it. In fact, in my twenties, I basically disowned my brother Boyd altogether. I loathed him so much! Then I became a Christian, and the Holy Spirit immediately began to clean up my sinful lifestyle (more on that in the next chapter). One night, as I was reading my Bible, I came across 1 John 4:20 which says, "Whoever claims to love God yet hates a brother or sister is a liar. For whoever does not love their brother and sister, whom they have seen, cannot love God, whom they have not seen" (NIV). It was at that moment I realized my hate for my brother Boyd was as sinful as his homosexuality, maybe more so. It was clear to me my hate for my brother really grieved the heart of God. After many years of silence and separation, I called my brother Boyd and had a lengthy conversation with him and asked him for forgiveness for my hate. As we reconciled, he too asked for forgiveness and shared his struggle with sin. When I read God's word in 1 John 4:20, I realized I was more concerned about what other people might think about me if they found out I had a homosexual brother than I was concerned about Boyd. It was always all about me and my pride—the mother of all sins. It's so deceptive and diabolical! My pride can sure make me feel good about myself when I can look down on others who struggle. And when I do, the Devil has me right where he wants me.

Jesus said, "Hypocrite! First get rid of the log in your own eye; then you will see well enough to deal with the speck in your friend's eye" (Matthew 7:5 NIV). Years ago, a very wise man named Dallas Willard shared at a conference I was attending that the "log" Jesus is talking about here is "the log of condemnation." I was so condemning to my brother that I lost all love for him. That's what condemnation does. It's wretched, and it's sin! My job as a Christ-follower is to love sinners like me and never condemn them. Be Jesus to them.

Did Boyd suddenly get "well" and become a heterosexual? No. He continued to struggle, but I loved him anyway. He stood up in my wedding in 1989, even though he struggled. And he struggled until his very young death from AIDS at the age of thirty-eight in 1995. I'm convinced he's in Heaven. He accepted Jesus as his Savior, even though he struggled with sin until the end.

One of the greatest Christ-followers of all time, the Apostle Paul, struggled with sin. Talking about his sin nature, he wrote, "For I have the desire to do what is good, but I cannot carry it out. For I do not do the good I want to do, but the evil I do not want to do—this I keep on doing" (Romans 7:18b-19 NIV). Have you ever felt that way? That is simply what it is to struggle with sin. Sin is our primary struggle in life. It may sound strange, but it's a good and worthwhile struggle.

Michael Allen, my best friend in seminary, says this about sin: "Sin will take you further than you want to go, keep you longer than you want to stay, and cost you more than you can afford to pay." That's some wisdom there. Struggle with it, but don't try to justify it. Justifying sin is all about pride. Pride is all about self-sufficiency instead of reliance upon God. At its core, pride says, "I am my own God." Believe me, you don't want to go there. And if you do, you can be sure you will not win. "God is opposed to the proud but gives grace to the humble" (1 Peter 5:5b NASB).

The key here is to get humble. I often pray, "Show me my sin, Lord!" And He does…and guess what? "If we confess our sins, he is faithful and just and will forgive us our sins and purify us from all unrighteousness" (1 John 1:9 NIV). That is called *grace*. Immediately after that list of ten sins we reviewed earlier from 1 Corinthians 6:9-10 is verse 11: "And that is what some of you *were*. But you were washed, you were sanctified, you were justi-fied in the name of the Lord Jesus Christ and by the Spirit of our God" (1 Corinthians 6:11 NIV). And that's exactly what I was too! But—and that's a big "But!"—followed by those words defin-ing such amazing grace: I was washed, sanctified, justified. Grace is *so* amazing it becomes the awesome subject matter of the next chapter.

I could ask how real sin is on Amir's scale. Or I could just sim-ply ask how real sin is in your life. Go ahead and circle one of the following.

A = Absolutely authentic.
B = Maybe authentic but questionable.
C = No way—pretty much all fabricated.

If you circled "A" like me, you're really going to appreciate the next chapter.

I'm really glad I'm finally at the end of this chapter. I want to be done with sin so badly. Don't you? God has provided a way.

five

Salvation

Have you seen the Marvel movie *Avengers: Infinity War*? If you haven't, this is a spoiler alert: All the Avenger superheroes show up to battle Thanos, whose intent is to destroy half the population in the universe to bring balance to the cosmos. By the end of the movie, he wins! Not only does half the population of the universe turn to dust, but half the Avengers do as well. Doctor Strange, Spider-Man, Black Panther, even Nick Fury, all disintegrate! Poof, gone! And the movie ends. *What?* How does evil Thanos *win*?

As I've already intimated, it's a bad movie when evil wins. But, if you follow the Avengers, and a large contingent of the planet seems to, here's the deal: We knew a sequel was coming. And what happens?—*spoiler alert again*—salvation! All the good guys who disappeared are resurrected and the effects of evil are overturned. Again, and again and again, what is so amazing about these Hollywood movies is how great they are at writing stories involving

71

salvation. This is because the idea of salvation is intrinsically in our hearts—so much so they will even resurrect heroes who are certain to be dead to come back and save the day! Marvel movies like this are simply made-up stories about a *real* story—*the* story—the ancient, true story of God and us.

Here's the truth: if we are just left with the consequences of our sin, then it's certain death—no hope! And that's bad news! If there was no sequel to *Avengers: Infinity War*, then that is ultimately a bad movie and a sad story. If there is no sequel for our life, that is the worst kind of bad news! But we know a sequel is coming. Here is the great news: God has a sequel for your life—a really *good* sequel—and it starts with Jesus!

One of Jesus' twelve disciples, named Thomas, said to Jesus, "Lord, we don't know where you are going, so how can we know the way?" (John 14:5 NIV) The word *way* in the original Greek language is *odus*. It means "road" or "way." Interestingly, God always provides humans with a road or a pathway out of misery. In fact, the title of the Old Testament book of Exodus means "road out," from *Ex,* meaning *out,* and *odus,* meaning *road/way.* For the Israelites enslaved in Egypt, the book of Exodus, written by Moses, catalogs the road or the way or the journey out of slavery. In response to Thomas' inquiry above, Jesus said something no other spiritual leader ever said: "Jesus answered, 'I am the way, the truth and the life, no one comes the father except through me'" (John 14:6 NIV).

Let's look at those words for a moment: "I am." Those two little words are the very words God used when He revealed to Moses who He was in Exodus, "God said to Moses, 'I AM WHO I AM. This is what you are to say to the Israelites: "I Am has sent me to you"'" (Exodus 3:14 NIV).

The "I am" words Jesus uses to respond to Thomas are Jesus clearly claiming He is God and that He, in fact, is *The Road* to salvation. Not "a" road, *The Road—The Way Out*! And to make it abundantly clear, Jesus says, "No one comes to the father except through me." This means Jesus is the *only* road to salvation; there is no other. And frankly, this is where people of other religions and even non-religious people get hung up at times. They say, "That's so exclusive. Aren't there are many paths to God? Jesus couldn't have really said that!" I respond that not only did Jesus absolutely *say* it, but He *had* to say it. Because only Jesus dealt with the primary problem of humanity in totality—Sin. Jesus not only died for all of our sins, but He was also raised from the dead and overcame death on that first Easter morning. No other religion claims to deal with human sin to the degree Jesus did, and that is exactly what authentic, historic Christianity claims.

A Brief Look at Other Major World Religions

Buddhism

The original Buddha was a guy named Siddhartha Gautama. He lived during the fifth century BC in China and was from a wealthy family. He was sheltered and protected from the poor and destitute living throughout China. When he left the protection of his home and actually witnessed firsthand the widespread suffering of the people, he was not moved to "save" everyone. Instead, he came up with a philosophy of sorts to deal with human suffering. Gautama himself was not concerned with Heaven or Hell or the human soul. In fact, he did not believe in an afterlife, or that human beings had souls. It wasn't until centuries later that a different strain of Buddhism emerged that, in a sense, made Buddha a god. Research it for yourself—his story is pretty wild. There is no ultimate salvation in the original Buddhist religion. Zen Buddhism, quite in vogue in the United States, is a form of meditative Buddhism that believes salvation comes from self. There are many forms of Buddhism today, even some that have some Christian elements, but none are definitively Christianity.

Islam, or the Muslim Religion

Islam is one of the world's youngest major religions. It goes back to the seventh century AD when Muhammad brought it forth in Mecca, Saudi Arabia. Muhammad claimed he had received a vision from God. He attempted to spread it peacefully, but when that didn't work, he used violence. He died around 632 AD. Muslims make no claims that Muhammed was sinless, as Jesus was. The fact is, the Quran states Jesus was the perfect prophet. But, they say, Muhammed was the greatest. The path to salvation for the Muslim is to follow the Five Pillars of Islam. If that doesn't work, there is the Sixth Pillar—Jihad, which is to engage in a Holy War. This is why some strains of the Islamic faith are so violent. I encourage you to learn a bit more on your own. But suffice it to say, ultimate salvation is pretty tenuous for Muslims.

Hinduism

Hindus embrace both a pantheistic and polytheistic version of religion. *Pan-* means "everything." *Poly-* means "many." That is to say, in Hinduism everything in the universe is God, and there are many gods. Because of this, it's hard to pin down exactly what Hindus believe, and like Buddhism there are many strains of Hinduism. Hinduism began around 3000 years ago, and in its early stages looked a lot like witchcraft. Early Hindus "worshipped a Mother Goddess and a horned god in the posture of yogi."[21] Karma and reincarnation are big for Hindus. Your moral character and your subsequent deeds or actions builds *karma*—your destiny resulting from the effects or consequences of what you do and who you are. The karma you build in one life can cause you to ascend or descend to a greater or lesser being in the next life, which can be an endless process. In some strains of Hinduism, Nirvana is reached through "the detachment from self and attachment to reality as a whole—a state of passionless peace."[22] The three stages of Yoga seek to achieve salvation: 1) by embracing the knowledge of the sages and Hindu scriptures; 2) through devotion to a manifestation of a chosen god; and 3) through works, performing ceremonies, sacrifices, pilgrimages, and other good deeds.[23] Ultimately good, bad, right, wrong, even sin, done and observed in the world, is an illusion. So, if one must be saved, the question is, saved from what? It's important to know the New Age movement, with its belief that all is one, is simply a modern version of ancient Hinduism!

Judaism, or the Jewish Faith

Christianity has its roots in the Jewish faith. The entire Old Testament of the Christian Bible is all about the Jewish faith. Jesus himself was a Jew. Many Jews of the Old Testament had a forward-looking faith in a coming Messiah. Other Jews of the Old Testament often got caught up in a legalistic faith, rigidly following the Ten Commandments and 613 Levitical laws. Moses was the purported recipient of the commandments and laws. Therefore, he and Elijah were considered the greatest prophets of the Old Testament and were revered by Jews for centuries, even today. Amazingly, in Luke 17 in a place known as the Mount of Transfiguration, Peter, James, and John went up the mountain with Jesus and it was there that both Moses and Elijah appeared with Jesus. Then, the voice of the Father said, "This is my son whom I love, listen to him." In other words, it was there and then God the Father made it abundantly clear Jesus trumped both Moses and Elijah. Many Jews have since put their faith in Jesus, their Messiah, but the majority still persist in the legalistic Levitical rituals or are Jews only in heritage.

Wicca

Wicca is a relatively new religion based upon old cults and pagan cultures which pre-date Christianity. It began in the United Kingdom in the 1940s and came to the United States in the 1960s. It has grown significantly in America, with over 800,000 people claiming to be adherents. Wicca is polytheistic in nature, celebrating both gods and goddesses. Nature is a very important aspect of Wicca, and magic is practiced for the purpose of doing good, with an emphasis on healing.

Wicca holds an appeal for many who desire a spiritual connection to nature, often personified as Mother Earth and Father Sky, with celebrations focused on the cycles of the moon and the sun. Recently an article was published in the *New York Times* titled, "400 Years Ago They Would Be Witches. Today They Can Be Your Coach." The article highlighted an ever-increasing desire for spiritual coaches in the United States. While not explicitly citing Wicca, many elements in the article aligned with Wicca or New Age. Many people have been turned off by organized religion. Others have been hurt. Still others are simply seeking to nurture their spiritual needs in a way that suits them. The primary creed of the Wiccan is: "Harm none and do as you will."[24] For those familiar with the Old Testament book of Judges, it's reminiscent of the very last verse of the entire book that reads, "In those days, Israel had no king. Everyone did what seemed right in their own eyes" (Judges 21:25 NLT). It's worth noting that in Wicca there seems to be no real thought of or desire for salvation. Instead, immediate spiritual gratification seems to be the primary goal.

Cultural Beliefism

If you have never heard of it, don't worry, I just made up the name. But you'll get it. I love culture and people of different ethnic backgrounds. I love all the different foods and many of the different cultural traditions. When I learn about and hang with people of different skin colors and ethnicities, I'm enriched. When I take teams on mission trips to Africa, I encourage everyone to take every opportunity to lean into the culture, the people, the food, and the traditions. However, in just about every culture, including American culture, people come up with spiritual and moral beliefs they follow. Some align with historic Christianity, some don't. Embrace the ones that do and throw out the ones that don't. However, beware! Often people of different cultures put forth beliefs you must follow…or else. In the United States, people post signs in their yards and display certain types of banners making it clear what they believe. Part of those beliefs are based on what the people displaying those banners and flags want others to believe about them. Some of those beliefs sound good on the surface and could even align with historic Christian beliefs, but when investigating what they really mean, they become quite problematic.

As a Christ-follower, often the culture tells me to believe things that are contrary to God's Word. Jesus said, "I am the way, the truth and the life" (John 14:6). And Jesus constantly pointed people to the Scriptures to ensure they were following the time-tested truths of God's word. In our country, and perhaps yours, there's a new mantra called, "Your Truth." You can do, be, and display whatever you want, "as long as it doesn't hurt others," very similar to Wicca. But here's the great irony: If I disagree with the prevailing cultural beliefs set forth by the media, a particular political party, many secular educational institutions, etc., it still seems to be okay, even proper, to slam historic Christianity, which for a guy like me is perplexing. In fact, if I state something against a cultural truth, I'm labeled a "hater." Even if I repented of my cultural waywardness, you would think all would be forgiven, but I'm not. I'm still suspected of hatefulness by the culture gods. This is the biggest problem with cultural beliefism, it saves no one and condemns many. Quite often, those who label people as haters for not complying with their cultural beliefism are more hateful than those whom they are trying to hang their "hater label" on.

It seems this is particularly true for devoted Christ-followers who won't comply.

Jesus warned and encouraged his followers of this tendency in His Sermon on the Mount:

"God blesses you when people mock you and persecute you and lie about you and say all sorts of evil things against you because you are my followers. Be happy about it! Be very glad! For a great reward awaits you in heaven. And remember, the ancient prophets were persecuted in the same way" (Matthew 5:11-12 NLT). In the very same chapter of Matthew, Jesus also commanded his followers to love our enemies. "But I say, love your enemies! Pray for those who persecute you! In that way, you will be acting as true children of your Father in heaven" (Matthew 5:44-45a NLT).

It is important to understand that everything about cultures is not a moral issue. We should embrace the positive aspects of various cultures, reject their immoral elements, and then be careful not to conform, be influenced by, or be negatively transformed by the practices which are immoral within those cultures. Our job as followers of Jesus is to influence and transform people and culture. Paul wrote in his letter to the Christians in Rome, "Do not conform to the pattern of this world but be transformed by the renewing of your mind. Then you will be able to test and approve what God's will is—his good, pleasing, and perfect will" (Romans 12:2 NIV).

One last very important note on cultural beliefism: we cannot, nor should not, expect people who don't know Jesus to act like they do know Jesus. Without Jesus, they do not have the Holy Spirit who gives us the power and desire to know and live God's word. Our job, as noted above, is to love people who don't know Jesus, even though their beliefs sometimes war against ours.

Be Wary of the -isms

Early in my spiritual journey, my pastor shared some wisdom that has stuck with me ever since: "Be wary of the *-isms*." Other religions have some truths. To paraphrase C.S. Lewis: Like arithmetic, some religions are closer to the right answer, but there is only one correct answer. His name is Jesus. The *-isms* can take you down many different roads which can bring a lot of confusion into your life, whether it's Buddhism, Hinduism, Taoism, or Cultural Beliefism. Even Christian Fundamentalism, which focuses on very legalistic tendencies, can cause a lot of damage. Check out all the other religions. All the other leaders. Do a thorough study. If you are open-minded and honest, I believe you will come to the same conclusion a Jew named Peter, Jesus' disciple, came to. He said, "Jesus is "'the stone you builders rejected, which has become the cornerstone." Salvation is found in no one else, for there is no other name under Heaven given to mankind by which we must be saved'" (Acts 4:11-12 NIV).

Did you get that? *No other name! Only Jesus!* "For there is one God and one Mediator who can reconcile God and humanity— the man Christ Jesus" (1 Timothy 2:5 NLT).

Here's the bottom line: Most other religions say that in order to be saved you need to follow our rules, obey our tenants, and increasingly be more religious according to our traditions and writings, even if you're not religious. It's do, do, do! A lot of people think, and a lot of religions teach, "If the good outweighs the bad—you're in!" But that is a lie! You can never know if you are good enough, and the reality is, no one is good enough. With all other religions, it's *do*. With Jesus, it's *done*! Jesus has done for us what we could never do for ourselves. No other name than Jesus—period!

The reality is this: Based on our own good deeds, good looks, good whatever, we will never make it to Heaven. Remember, all have sinned and fall short. Here are a few questions to consider: Do you believe God is good? I hope so. Do you believe a good God would want to keep us guessing whether we, his children, would make it home to Heaven? No good parent would say to their son as they sent him off to school, "Charlie, if you're good in school today and pay attention, you might be able to eat dinner and sleep in your bed at home. If not, you are out on the street tonight, hungry, and cold!" What good mom or dad would then let Charlie worry all day whether he's been good enough to have a meal and a bed that night? That is a terrible parent who should be reported to child protective services, and that's certainly not the good God of the Bible either. Jesus constantly spoke of how good his Father is. He said, "You parents—if your children ask for a loaf of bread, do you give them a stone instead? Or if they ask for a fish, do you give them a snake? Of course not! So if you sinful people know how to give good gifts to your children, how much more will your Heavenly Father give good gifts to those who ask him" (Matthew 7:9-11 NLT).

How much more indeed? If it's up to us to rely on our own goodness, then all we can do is hope we're good enough and we'll never know for sure. However, if we commit to rely on God and trust Him, we can be absolutely sure! God is so, so good, He offers us grace. That word *grace* literally means *undeserved favor.* You can never earn it; you can never pay for it. And the only way to receive it is to humbly admit your need for it. You, me, we utterly need grace! And our good Father offers it to anyone who wants it. The Bible says, "By grace you are saved, though faith—and this is not from yourselves, it is a gift of God—not by works, so that no one can boast" (Ephesians 2:8-9 NLT).

I shared that verse with my friend Paul, who grew up Catholic. He said, "My Catholic Bible doesn't say that." I said, "I bet it does!" So, he ran next door to his house, grabbed his big old flower-pressing Catholic Bible, brought it over, and we opened that baby up to these verses, and guess what? While it is a different translation, it said this almost exactly to the word! He said, "They didn't teach me this growing up and when I was an altar boy!" And shortly after that, he made a focused commitment to surrender to Christ and receive God's grace. And His grace is not exclusive—it's inclusive! Jesus wants to include everyone. "The Lord is not slow in keeping his promise, as some understand slowness. Instead he is patient with you, not wanting anyone to perish, but everyone to come to repentance" (2 Peter 3:9 NIV). God wants none to perish! He will do everything necessary for you to be saved, but one thing He won't do is violate your free will.

Repentance—Our Small, Simple Humble Part

God has done everything to give every person salvation. But you and I have one very small role to play, and it takes humility. It's called repentance. It literally means to turn around and turn back to God. How do we do it? It is simply crying out to God, "God, forgive me, I need you!" That's it! You may ask: Who won't be saved? The simple answer is: Those who refuse to repent. I cover this in greater detail in the chapter on Hell. One of the greatest things I have learned over many years in my walk with Jesus came from the great evangelist, Billy Graham. I remember watching him be interviewed when he was around 90 years old—he lived to 99. He was asked something like, "Reverend Graham, so many TV evangelists have fallen through scandal over the decades, but you somehow have maintained your integrity. How?" His answer penetrated deep into my bones and my soul. He replied, "I have simply tried to live a lifestyle of daily repentance." A lifestyle of repentance—daily repentance. Wow! That lifestyle takes ongoing humility. "God opposes the proud but gives grace to the humble" (James 4:6 ESV). I could easily insert this paragraph below into the section on sanctification because I believe it's paramount for ongoing sanctification. Repent to God once for all your sins to secure your place in Heaven, then live a daily lifestyle of repentance to live in the kingdom of God on Earth, as Billy Graham did.

Reject Universalism

Sometimes our human emotions mess with our theology. We want everyone to be saved so much that some Christians have adopted a theological construct for salvation called Universalism. What Universalism says is, when Jesus died on the cross he paid for everyone's sins and therefore everyone who ever lived will be in Heaven, and none will go to Hell. This is a twisting of the Scriptures and neglects a great many passages in the Bible. Universalism ultimately violates our free will, because by simple reasoning it requires that all people spend an eternity with God—even those who rejected him! This is like God forcing us to love Him, and God does not do that. We will discuss this further in the chapter on Hell. Universalism sounds great on the surface, intimating that we can all live according to our own truth, but in the end there is no truth in it!

Salvation is a transaction between God and us where He's done everything. We have one simple little role to play where we exercise our free will to trust Christ and ask him for forgiveness. If you haven't done so, now is the time to exercise that free will! Can we just pause right here and go to God right now and tell God we need Him? Perhaps get down your knees and humbly say this very simple prayer to God right now:

> *"God, forgive me for all my sins, save me, Jesus, I need You! I believe in You. I surrender to You today!"*

That's it. If you said those words right now and really meant them, you are saved! So, so good! That's the best news ever! And know this: with God, when you surrender, you win! You win paradise forever! It's so good, and it's great to further understand the depth of the good news and who it's for.

The Depth of The Good News

The Apostle Paul wrote, "You see, at just the right time, when we were still powerless, Christ died for the ungodly. Very rarely will anyone die for a righteous person, though for a good person someone might possibly dare to die. But God demonstrates his own love for us in this: While we were still sinners, Christ died for us" (Romans 5:6-8 NIV).

Friends, that's such good news! We were done! Doomed! Powerless! We had no energy to do good deeds, unable to reach out to God. When we were at our very worst, what happened? Christ

died for us! Then the first two words of verse 8, "But God!" *But…
God!* That's such a *big but!* But God so greatly demonstrated His
own love for us in this amazing act—that while we were still sinners…lost…Christ died for us!

Back in the days of Christ, the Romans ruled the known world.
Prior to the Romans, the Greeks, led by Alexander the Great, conquered the Mediterranean from Greece to Egypt, and eastward to
India. Part of his plan of conquest was to "Hellenize"—or make
Greek—every country and culture he conquered, requiring them to
thoroughly adopt the Greek culture and language. This was done so
effectively that even centuries later, though Latin was the Romans'
native tongue, most of the Roman Empire spoke Greek, even the
Roman soldiers. The ancient Greek word for "good news" was *euaggelion.* When the Roman armies won a battle, they'd ride back into
Rome and shout "Euaggelion, Euaggelion!"[25] If it had been English,
they would have shouted, "Good news, good news! Victory!
Victory!" In the Bible, when the angel appeared to the shepherds
and announced the birth of Christ, they were afraid, "But the angel
said to them, 'Do not be afraid. I bring you good news (euaggelion)
that will cause great joy for all the people'" (Luke 2:10 NIV). The
Messiah, the Lord, had come, and it was indeed *Good News!*

God has such good news for us…for you. We need to understand the heart of God. Way back around 750 BC, God inspired
the prophet Micah to write, "Who is a God like you, who pardons
sin and forgives the transgressions of the remnant of his inheri-
tance? You do not stay angry forever but delight to show mercy"
(Micah 7:18 NIV). God pardons sin, forgives, and delights to show
mercy. That is remarkably Good News, but there is more. The
Good News provides reconciliation between humans and God.

Reconciliation

When a word shows up in successive verses in the Bible, it's clear God is trying to make a point. In Romans chapter 5, *reconciliation* is one of those keywords. The Apostle Paul wrote,

> "Since we have now been justified by his blood, how much more shall we be saved from God's wrath through him! For if, while we were God's enemies, we were *reconciled* to him through the death of his Son, how much more, having been *reconciled*, shall we be saved through his life! Not only is this so, but we also boast in God through our Lord Jesus Christ, through whom we have now received *reconciliation*" (Romans 5:9-11 NIV, *italics added*).

The way *reconciliation* is being used in the passage, think of it in terms of accounting, like reconciling your checkbook, bringing it into balance. We are out of balance with God. Sin has placed us deep in debt. We're in the negative. We need reconciliation, but our debt is too great to make it right on our own. So great, in fact, that only God can bring our accounting back into balance. God loves to show mercy, and His mercy and grace are delivered by Jesus, who paid the price on the cross to reconcile your account. That is Good News.

We long for reconciliation, but often we try to reconcile our misdeeds on our own, without God. We pass the blame: "Oh, if she wouldn't have done that, I wouldn't have done this." We deflect: "She is so much worse than me!" We deny: "It is really sin?" It's all a misguided attempt to reconcile our own moral accounting. We can't do it on our own. We need God.

At this point, as you read, perhaps you should take a pause and consider that God has a sequel for your life. We begin on the path of *Avengers: Infinity Wars*, where evil dominates—the end. But in the sequel, *Avengers: Endgame*, the heroes are resurrected, and evil is defeated. The Devil caused sin to come into this world, and sin brought death—the end. But God had a sequel, the continuation of the story, and the resurrection of Jesus defeated the Devil and conquered sin. The sequel sets things right. It reconciles your account. It brings you from death to life.

You may be asking, "What do I need to do?" Answer: Thank Him. Thank Jesus for His mercy, grace, and love. That's it. Say something like this to God in prayer:

"Dear Lord Jesus, thank you for paying the price for my sins by dying on the cross and reconciling my moral books. Thank you for your mercy and grace by forgiving me of all my sins. Thank you for rising from the grave, which gives me hope for a magnificent sequel for my life, forever with You. Amen."

If you said that prayer and really meant it, that's amazing! God has great things ahead for you! One of those great things is this: God wants to enlist you as one of His emissaries. It is as though He says, "Now that you have been reconciled, I want to use you to help Me reconcile others." Think about that for a moment. If God has zeroed out your spiritual account and made you right with

Him, then there could be nothing more important than helping others be reconciled to Him as well. So, He gives us a new redemptive perspective of other people. The verses below are the marching orders for all Christ-followers:

> "So, from now on we regard no one from a worldly point of view. Though we once regarded Christ in this way, we do so no longer. Therefore, if anyone is in Christ, the new creation has come: The old has gone, the new is here! All this is from God, who reconciled us to himself through Christ and gave us the ministry of reconciliation: that God was reconciling the world to himself in Christ, not counting people's sins against them. And he has committed to us the message of reconciliation" (2 Corinthians 5:16-19 NIV).

I could take up the rest of this book unpacking these incredible words from God to us. "We regard no one from a worldly point of view." This means God has a magnificent sequel for everyone. And He gives us a heavenly directive, a ministry in which God longs to use us to reconcile everyone we meet to Him. It's called discipleship. I wrote a whole book called *GROW* on the subject of discipleship because it is so vital! God gives us a lead role in the sequel of every person we meet who doesn't yet know God. It is incredible that God wants to use us in this way.

We are called to enter into people's lives, people who are down and out, people who are hopeless, people who have just been dumped, fired, flunked, kicked to the curb, or have made enormous mistakes. God asks us to show up in their lives, to be carriers of His love, mercy, and grace and say to them, "Euaggelion! Good News! God has an incredible sequel to your life! This is not the end of the story!"

The year was 2006. Amber Cloe, my goddaughter and niece, was just 21 years old and recently wed. Life was so full of promise for her. Then, she abruptly died of an overdose. She was my brother Brett's only child and he was destroyed! I went over to his house to console him. Being a pastor, I figured this is what God trained me for, but I couldn't have been more rocked when Brett flew into a rage and said, "God? Don't give me any of your God!" And that began a five-year journey of silence and separation between Brett and me. He wanted nothing to do with me or God. After all, in his heart and mind, I represented the very One who took away all that was near and dear to him. I felt rejected like never before.

After about five years, Brett and I began to talk a bit—small talk mostly. Every now and then we'd have some good conversations, but nothing too deep. Around that five-year mark, I read a book that helped me understand the devastation of losing a child at a far deeper level than I ever understood before. How could I really know? I've never lost a child. So, I sent him the book with a note asking him for forgiveness for my insensitivity. He responded favorably. Our relationship, while not what it once was, was amiable and better. I continued to hope and pray for more.

Fast-forward twelve years. Brett sent me an invitation to his wedding. He did not ask me to officiate the wedding, but I wasn't hurt by that. I was just overjoyed to be attending the celebration. Early one morning, I was meeting Bryce, another of my brothers.

Bryce says to me, "Brett's coming. He wants to ask you to do the wedding." Really? I was totally surprised. Sure enough, Brett shows up. "Brad, think you could officiate my wedding?" "Sure, I guess." Then without prompting, Brett tells me about his first wedding. "Yeah, I'll never forget that first wedding, Bradley. It was at a justice of the peace in California. Amber was two, I show up, and her mom was there. My bride says to me, 'Brett, when we go up to that altar, there will be no God, no Bible, and no Jesus!'" Then Brett says to me, "Bradley, right there and then I should have walked out because I lost my faith, and when Amber died, I really needed it." Sensing the moment, I asked Brett, "So, if I do your wedding, can I mention God, the Bible, and Jesus?" Without hesitation, Brett proclaims, "Hell, yes!" I wept! Euaggelion! Good News!

A few weeks later, I officiated Brett's wedding to Kathey aboard his boat, *Amber Cloe*, in Pacific City on the Oregon Coast. I mentioned God, had a Bible, and shared how Amber put her faith in Jesus at a beach just down the coast when she was fourteen. I also proclaimed the Good News to Brett, Kathey, and all who were there, many who didn't know Jesus yet. It was so good, perhaps the best wedding I've ever done! A number of Brett's mostly non-church-going friends came up to me and told me how it touched them deeply. Euaggelion! Good News! There really is nothing better. The Bible says all the angels of Heaven rejoice when one sinner repents and turns back to God and is reconciled to Him. Reconciliation is so good, no matter how long it takes!

In this life, division, separation, and even divorce happen. It is always painful. If you are in a divided marriage, know that you and the person you are separated from are of great worth to God!

If we, as Christ-followers, have been reconciled to God, we are not to condemn others. We are to fight for and wait for reconciliation. Second Corinthians 5:19 says that we are not to count people's sins against them, which means we are not to condemn them. A while back God gave me these words: *Condemnation is easy, redemption is hard!*

We live in a world where it seems everyone, everywhere is condemning others. The media and news are filled with condemnation. Our politics, both sides, are filled with condemnation. Social media is filled with condemnation. The Apostle Paul lamented about how the struggle of sin is so hard, but because of the salvation Jesus provides to all who trust in Him, he would not face God's condemnation. He wrote: "Therefore, there is now no condemnation for those who are in Christ Jesus" (Romans 8:1 NIV). There's a double meaning here. First, if Jesus is your Savior, you have escaped the ultimate condemnation—you're saved from Hell. Second, there should be no condemnation *in* you. This means that as Christ-followers we should never condemn others. It's not our job. Remember, condemnation is easy, redemption is hard!

God has done the hard work of reconciliation to redeem us. Jesus went all the way to the cross and died the worst death ever invented on a blood-stained cross. Then He invites us to be His partner in the most purposeful endeavor this side of Heaven. He gives us the ministry of reconciliation. If we have been forgiven of so much, and given such a heavenly calling to help others be reconciled to God, why would we choose to condemn others and kick them to the curb, regardless of what they have done?

The world says, "If someone does something wrong, disassociate yourself from them. Condemn them. It's all about self-preservation!" Someone tweets something foul or posts something unpopular and—*Boom!*—they are canceled or fired. It is easy, even acceptable, to condemn others for their failures. But that is not the way of the ministry of reconciliation. Our heavenly calling should exemplify love and forgiveness. So be very careful what you tweet or post on social media. Your condemnation of others may really be you condemning yourself. Jesus said, "For by your words you will be acquitted, and by your words you will be condemned" (Matthew 12:37 NIV). Besides, it is hard to be openly condemning toward someone, and then be taken seriously when you are trying to share God's love.

If you are the recipient of those condemning tweets and post, or being attacked while showing a genuine, humble love toward others, don't let it worry you. Jesus never worried about what other people thought of Him while He hung out with messy sinners and prostitutes. He didn't take it personally when people insulted him or challenged him. Even when Jesus was condemned to die on the cross, he remained silent, providing an example for us to follow (1 Peter 2:21).

No Judgment

Jesus took all the judgment meant for us on the cross. He was condemned to die for us. This means that when we die, for everyone who puts their faith in Jesus and receives his forgiveness, there will be no judgment seat moment where God will decide if we go to Heaven or Hell. It's already done because of Jesus. We are saved! The Apostle Paul writes: "He is the one who has rescued us from the terrors of the coming judgment" (1 Thessalonians 1:10b NLT).

Justification

When Jesus died on the cross, a cosmic theological legal transaction happened in God's court of law. It's called *justification*. It's actually a real legal term used in the court system, often used to justify a crime committed to free a person of guilt. In God's court, justification happens only through Jesus paying the legal debt we owe. Remember the following verse from the last chapter: "Therefore, since we have been justified through faith, we have peace with God through our Lord Jesus Christ" (Romans 5:1 NIV).

As I stated in the chapter on the Holy Trinity regarding atonement, specifically in the section titled "Penal Substitution," Jesus paid the legal debt we owed. When we believe in His substitutionary death on the cross on our behalf, He justifies us before God. He wipes our slate clean. Justification makes us a hundred percent sinless before God. Because of Jesus, God the Father looks at us from His judgment seat and pronounces us *not guilty*. That is amazing! As my friend Ray Noah said, "On the cross, Jesus pardoned your sin, removed your guilt, expunged your record, and made his righteousness yours. You now stand before God justified, just as if you've never sinned." That captures justification beautifully.

We love justification for ourselves and for those we lead to Christ, but often we have a hard time when it involves the sin of someone who we have trusted and may even worked with. I lead a group called EPIC Global Missions and we plant churches in Africa. I was struggling with a very difficult situation, where a ministry partner in Africa was going through a hard time and made some foolish mistakes. It was a very painful and complicated situation. Another ministry leader, who I didn't know very well but knew my struggling friend, said to me, "Brad, you just need to get rid of him. This will not reflect well on EPIC." I understood that and I didn't want any blemishes on our organization, but I still deeply loved this hurting African friend and didn't want to kick him to the curb. While I was processing the difficulty of all this with my then eighteen-year-old son, Nathan, he said to me, "Dad, I heard once at a youth conference: 'Jesus never was concerned with being guilty by association!'" That was the truth I needed to hear. Jesus lived and died to justify us and was concerned with redemption and reconciliation and *salvation*. He is the God who delights in mercy and grace and reconciliation. So good!

The great irony of many Christian leaders is that they preach a message of grace, but they behave like the religious leaders of Jesus' day who were full of judgment and condemnation. Too many churches are turning their people into Christian Pharisees. It is the complete opposite of what Jesus intended, and it is unfortunate. God desires to transform our *mess* into His *message* of grace, love, and hope, because God is in the redemption business. He longs to redeem, reconcile, and sanctify everyone!

What my ministry partner in Africa needed—and what we all need—is to lean into the love and grace of Jesus and trust Him, allowing the Holy Spirit to clean us up, a little or a lot. What is amazing is that my ministry partner *did* receive some correction, and God is still using him to advance His kingdom in Africa.

Once Jesus redeems us, justifies us, and reconciles us, the Holy Spirit begins to clean us up, then He uses us increasingly for His glory. That's called *sanctification*. It's a key part of our Salvation story.

Sanctification: The word means to be holy or be made holy. It has two parts, both *immediate* and *ongoing*. After listing ten different sins, most of which the majority of us have committed, the Apostle Paul wrote: "And that is what some of you were. But you were washed, you were sanctified, you were justified in the name of the Lord Jesus Christ and by the Spirit of our God" (1 Corinthians 6:11 NIV).

Immediate Sanctification: The writer of Hebrews wrote, "And by that will, we have been made holy through the sacrifice of the body of Jesus Christ once for all" (Hebrews 10:10 NIV). When we put our faith in Christ, we are immediately sanctified, which means we are made pure, good to go, ready for Heaven, and guaranteed eternal life. All of this is done through the blood sacrifice of Jesus Christ on the cross.

When we hear and believe the Good News we can shout, "Euaggelion!" Here is more good news: The Holy Spirit invades our souls and seals us with a guarantee of our entrance to Heaven! It's a free pass into paradise.

When Jesus saves us, the Holy Spirit *immediately* sanctifies us—makes us holy—but then He continues to make us *more* holy on a daily basis.

Ongoing Sanctification: Sanctification, the process of being made holy, is also *ongoing.* Christ-followers long to become holy like Jesus, but it doesn't just happen instantaneously when we first put our faith in Him. I am convinced that being the most Holy person is not being the most moral person. Yes, moral integrity is part of the sanctification process, but Christianity is not moralism (Alert! There's another *-ism*). Many other faith systems have good morality, and even atheists can be moral. Christianity is about doing life with the *most* moral person to ever walk the planet and learning to love as He loved. I tell my kids, "You are, or eventually become, whoever you hang out with." Hang out with Jesus. When people—really messy people—hung out with Jesus, they were radically transformed and sanctified. It still happens today, and they all become more loving as a result. While morality may be part of what it means to be holy, if we emphasize morality over love in regard to what it means to become holy, we will likely end up like the religious leaders of Jesus' day, very judgmental and spiritually unattractive. To be holy, literally means *to be set apart*. When God makes us holy, he sets us apart for his work. We are to be different. Very different.

Here's my description of holiness: *The most holy person in the room is the person most willing to love the most unholy person.* The most holy person will love and show compassion to the most unholy, the wretched, the *stinkiest*. That is so different, isn't it? The most holy person loves the unlovable. That's what Jesus did, and He did it for me.

The most central element of our ongoing sanctification is to grow in love.

"Always be humble and gentle. Be patient with each other, making allowance for each other's faults because of your love" (Ephesians 4:2 NLT).

This is my current life verse. I sure want people to make an allowance for my faults. Don't you? Here God calls me to make an allowance for others' faults; to love them anyway. It begins a whole new awesome chapter—a new sequel for your life, and for someone else's too. Are you interested?

God has a Sequel for You!

How do you get into the theater showing your Salvation movie? Well, there is a ticket, and it has already been paid for by Jesus. It's called repentance. Simply saying to God, "Jesus, forgive me, save me, change me!" That's it.

Here's the crazing thing: Do you remember Thanos? He did the worst thing he could possibly do—he annihilated half the population of the planet (of the universe!). That's fiction of course. In reality though, 2000 years ago, humanity did the worst possible thing we could have done—kill God! We killed Jesus by hanging him on a cross. Jesus' disciples thought it was over, but it wasn't! Three days later Jesus rose from the dead and the ultimate sequel was announced by angels to women who first saw Him: "He has risen!". It changed everything. God took the worst thing we ever did and turned it into the best thing that has ever happened in human history. It is the sequel of Jesus' resurrection. This sequel has resurrected countless lives over the centuries. God has written a part for you to play in this sequel, because His sequel is your sequel.

Have you embraced the salvation Jesus offers? How authentic is what He did for you in your life? On Amir's scale I give it an "A." But circle how much you believe in the salvation Jesus offers:

A = Absolutely authentic.
B = Maybe authentic but questionable.
C = No way—pretty much all fabricated.

If you circled A, then if you don't already know, Jesus is calling you to get in the salvation game. That is why He saves us and leaves most of us here, so we can share the Good News with others who desperately need Him too.

It's the greatest sequel. God gave me a sequel, and it has been sensational: a beautiful wife, ridiculously joyous kids, and deep friendship! I've seen the world through missions, and all over the planet many people have a common denominator in Jesus our Savior. But not everyone knows Him yet. Some, like me before I met Jesus, are headed for an eternity in Hell. That's the subject of the next chapter.

six

Hell

The most dreaded call ever! I have received *the call* several times over the years, but none was more poignant than when my niece, Amber, died in August of 2006, almost exactly one year after the death of my brother Bryan. Both died of complications from drugs and alcohol, untimely deaths that could have been avoided. I was filled with grief and shock. Have you ever received *the call?*

If you live long enough it is sure to happen—someone you love will die. It fills you with unspeakable grief. When you share it with someone, they often offer the standard fare of consolation: "He's in a better place, she's at peace now." We all hope for Heaven. Most people, no matter their religion—and even many atheists—secretly hope that after this life they'll go to Heaven or some form of paradise, or at the very least, "a better place."

You may be familiar with the saying, "There are two truths in this life: death and taxes." While you may be able to skip out on your taxes, you can be assured that at some point you will die. The question is, after death...what? What eternal fate can a person truly expect? According to an accurate read of the Bible, there are only two options: Heaven or Hell.

Purgatory

Some of our Catholic friends believe in a place called Purgatory—something of a holding place until you have been *purged* of your remaining sin, or someone still living bails you out. During the Dark Ages, the Catholic church actually employed people to go around selling "spiritual items" or requesting direct monetary gifts that would pardon someone's sin or limit a relative's stay in Purgatory. But is Purgatory even real? Not according to the sixty-six books of the Bible—thirty-nine Old Testament books and twenty-seven New Testament books—recognized by the historic Protestant church. Understand this: the Catholic Bible traditionally has seventy-three books—forty-six in the Old Testament and twenty-seven in the New Testament. One of the extra books in the Catholic Old Testament books is Second Maccabees, which alludes to the idea of Purgatory as Judas Maccabeus prayed for his dead friends. Even though it says he didn't expect them to be saved, it says, "Thus he made atonement for the dead that they might be absolved from their sin." Because of this passage, as well as a few others in the additional Catholic texts, many Catholic leaders have taught that a place like Purgatory exists to give people a chance after their death. Based upon my personal study of the Bible, I cannot believe that to be true. Just to be clear, on Amir's scale I give Purgatory a C: there is no way that it is true.

Jesus supplies his own contradiction of Purgatory in Luke chapter 16 in verses 16-31. When I was in seminary, I had a deep conversation about this with a fellow classmate named Michael. I told him, "God will give people another chance to accept Jesus after they die." Michael challenged me to search the Scriptures and to show him where I find that in God's Word. I could not. But I did find this passage which clearly shows that after a person dies their eternal resting place is fixed—forever. Let's go through the passage with a bit of commentary.

These are the words of Jesus:

> "There was a rich man who was dressed in purple and fine linen and lived in luxury every day. At his gate was laid a beggar named Lazarus, covered with sores and longing to eat what fell from the rich man's table. Even the dogs came and licked his sores. The time came when the beggar died, and the angels carried him to Abraham's side. The rich man also died and was buried. In Hades, where he was in torment, he looked up and saw Abraham far away, with Lazarus by his side" (Luke 16:19-23 NIV).

We read here that Lazarus, the beggar, dies, and we can safely assume the place the Angels carried him to was Heaven. There is no doubt that's where Abraham was. The rich man died too. He landed in Hades, the Greek name for Hell. That establishes both Heaven and Hell as landing places for the deceased. Look what happens next as the true story continues:

"So he called to him, 'Father Abraham, have pity on me and send Lazarus to dip the tip of his finger in water and cool my tongue, because I am in agony in this fire'" (Luke 16:24 NIV).

In Hell, the rich man calls up to Abraham. He is in agony in the heat of Hell, and he wants Abraham to send Lazarus with a drink of water. Incredibly, the rich man imagines he still has some pull or authority based upon his former status in life, wanting Lazarus to serve his needs. See how Abraham responds:

"But Abraham replied, 'Son, remember that in your lifetime you received your good things, while Lazarus received bad things, but now he is comforted here and you are in agony. And besides all this, between us and you a great chasm has been set in place, so that those who want to go from here to you cannot, nor can anyone cross over from there to us'" (Luke 16:25-26 NIV).

Even if Abraham wanted to go comfort someone in Hell, he couldn't. A great chasm has been fixed in place between Heaven and Hell that no one can cross over from one side to the other. Ever the negotiator, the rich man asked Abraham a few last favors:

"He answered, 'Then I beg you, father, send Lazarus to my family, for I have five brothers. Let him warn them, so that they will not also come to this place of torment'" (Luke 16:27-28 NIV).

Though he still wants Lazarus to serve his desires, at least for once his focus is off himself. In desperation, the rich man pleads for the sake of his brothers that someone might warn them so they won't end up in this horrific place.

> "Abraham replied, 'They have Moses and the Prophets; let them listen to them.'
>
> "'No, Father Abraham,' he said, 'but if someone from the dead goes to them, they will repent.'
>
> "He said to him, 'If they do not listen to Moses and the Prophets, they will not be convinced even if someone rises from the dead'" (Luke 16:31 NIV).

Abraham points to the Bible, specifically the Old Testament, telling the rich man that his brothers already have "Moses and the Prophets" to provide them with all of the truth and warnings they need. Jesus, the narrator of this story, is also pointing to himself, for he would raise from the dead, and even then, many would not be convinced, even to this day.

Jesus uses this story of the rich man and Lazarus to make it clear that the Good News has been available from the beginning to those seeking God. But in order to get to Heaven and avoid Hell, one must accept Jesus in this life.

Highway to Hell

In 1986, I went to a church in Portland, Oregon, to support a friend recovering from drug addiction. She said she found Jesus.

Skeptical of her conversion, I went to make sure it wasn't a cult, though back then I really would not have known the difference. As the pastor ended his message, he asked everyone who wanted to receive Jesus as their Lord and Savior to stand up. To this day, I don't remember a word of his message, but I heard the voice of Jesus speak to my spirit almost audibly, "Brad, if you don't stand up right now, you're going to Hell in a handbasket."

At that point in my life, I didn't know any of the Bible, and certainly none of what I have written in this book. What I did know was that what I heard from God in that moment was true, and that it would be fair and just on His part if I went to Hell. I also knew that Hell was most definitely *not* where I wanted to spend eternity. And don't let this be lost: Jesus didn't force me into Heaven or Hell. It was my choice to hear his warning and accept it or reject it. So, I stood up and committed my life to Jesus. Those words Jesus spoke to my spirit were the single most loving words I could have ever heard. He spoke in a language I could understand, and He saved me from eternal damnation.

Think of your life as a dot and an arrow that goes on forever:

The dot is this life. The arrow is eternal life. Jesus makes it so clear: we will spend eternity in one of two places, Heaven, or Hell. The choice is not his, it's ours. Jesus honestly doesn't send anyone *to* Hell, He saves us *from* Hell. Track with these words from Jesus:

"For God did not send his Son into the world to condemn the world, but to save the world through him. Whoever believes in him is not condemned, but whoever does not believe stands condemned already because they have not believed in the name of God's one and only Son" (John 3:17).

This is a massive truth! Jesus doesn't condemn us. We already stand condemned to Hell. As the AC/DC rock and roll song goes, we're on a "Highway to Hell." Without Jesus, every man, woman, and child are on it. Our only hope is Jesus, and Jesus, in his deep love for us, warned us many times about the reality of Hell. In seven different passages of the Gospels, Jesus spoke of a place where there would be "weeping and gnashing of teeth." Here are a few:

"The Son of Man will send out his angels, and they will weed out of his kingdom everything that causes sin and all who do evil. They will throw them into the blazing furnace, where there will be weeping and gnashing of teeth" (Matthew 13:41-42 NIV).

"There will be weeping there, and gnashing of teeth, when you see Abraham, Isaac and Jacob and all the prophets in the kingdom of God, but you yourselves thrown out" (Luke 13:28 NIV).

Again, there are five other verses in the Gospels where Jesus uses the words, "weeping and gnashing of teeth," and all of them are about Hell.

Is Hell Real?

If you watch *The Walking Dead* series on zombies, that's kind of what Hell will be like. As much God desires none to perish (2 Peter 3:9), and as much I would rather not believe in Hell, I am convinced by God's word in Scripture, specifically the words of Jesus, that Hell is real, and some people will spend all eternity there.

Here are some statistics from a Pew Research Poll conducted in the United States in 2015 based on the question, "Is Hell real?"[26]:

58 percent of Americans believe in Hell
76 percent of Muslims believe in Hell
22 percent of Jews believe in Hell

Interestingly, there is a group called "Nones" which includes Atheists, Agnostics, or just non-religious people—people not connected to any religion (numbering approximately 271,000 in southwest Portland, who we are trying to reach).

27 percent of "Nones" believe in Hell

It is crazy that there are people who don't believe in God or aren't sure what to believe about God or faith or religion, yet they still have a believe that there is a Hell.

To be clear, just because a person believes in Hell doesn't make it real. Who is the ultimate authority on Hell? You might think it was the Devil. You could ask him all about it, but he would just lie to you anyway. His great deception to the masses is that he's not even real, and that Hell isn't real either. What a great strategy to deceive so many. But as we have seen above, Jesus is clear that Hell is real. The reality is, the Devil himself will spend eternity in Hell. And contrary to popular culture, he will not be the warden, but the chief inmate, bound and tormented forever. He will be satisfied with nothing less that to take as many people with him as he can. So who are you going to believe, Jesus or the Devil?

Who Will End Up in Hell?

So many people believe in Hell, but how many have asked the question: "Who will end up in Hell?" That is a great question to ask! We find some clear answers in the book of Revelation.

Remember, God desires none to perish. When love and kindness and an outpouring of gifts and goodness from God doesn't draw a person to Him, God will often use very difficult events to change a person's heart. Ideally, once we are faced with the greatness of God, whether in blessing or difficulty, we will acknowledge Him, repent, and seek His forgiveness.

Consider a man who has a heart attack. After his brush with death, he begins to exercise regularly, eat much healthier food, and embarks on other good behaviors which, had he engaged in previously he might have avoided that heart attack. This is a form of repentance from his former, unhealthy ways. Heart attacks and other life-altering ailments have drawn many wayward souls to consider their mortality and find true repentance in Jesus.

Now consider that same man who, after his heart attack, chooses to do nothing different. He avoids exercise and eats even greasier foods than before. His life is not altered. There is no change. We cannot be surprised when he succumbs to a second heart attack. He received a warning, but he just doesn't care. He is without excuse. When faced with the choice between life and death, he has chosen unwisely.

In Alcoholics Anonymous we used to say, "When you hit your bottom, you'll change—unless you die first." What does "the bottom" look like? It may be something different for each of us. A DUI, a spouse bringing home divorce papers, bankruptcy, rejection, a jail term, and even a heart attack. A really cataclysmic, painful event can be the best thing that ever happened to us. God will bring us to our most broken place so we can wake up and see the light—and repent. The more we refuse him, the further He goes to get our attention. Sometimes the most loving thing God can do is pour out His wrath.

This is what we see in the book of Revelation. God has made himself known to the world. The world has been faced with the life-altering decision of choosing sin. Acknowledge God and repent, or refuse to make any change, even in the face of God's greatness. Their choice is to refuse Him, and beginning in Revelation chapter 9, God begins to thrust His greatness upon them in what the Bible calls *wrath* or *plagues*. Even though these events are punitive, God is even still giving them every opportunity repent and turn to Him. In the end, they, too, will have no excuse. Here is how the Bible describes what happens next:

In Revelation chapter 9, verse 2, God sends "smoke, like that from a giant furnace." Then in verse 3, God sends locusts that were like scorpions which stung people and put them in such agony, that in verse 6 it says, "In those days people will seek death but will not find it. They will long to die, but death will flee from them" (Revelation 9:6 NLT). Imagine being in such pain and agony that you want to die, but you can't!

In verse 18, we are told one-third of all the people on the earth are, in fact, killed by three plagues. For those who survive, we see their response in verses 20 and 21: "But the people who did not die in these plagues still *refused to repent* of their evil deeds and turn to God. They continued to worship demons and idols made of gold, silver, bronze, stone, and wood—idols that can neither see nor hear nor walk! And *they did not repent* of their murders or their witchcraft or their sexual immorality or their thefts" (Revelation 9:20-21 NLT, *italics added*).

To answer the question, "Who will end up in Hell?" Everyone who does not repent! Those people who ultimately exercise their God-given free will to reject God will be excluded from Heaven and end up in Hell. Once again, they are without excuse. If that's not enough, keep reading the book of Revelation. We see repeatedly how God sends pain upon people so they might repent and turn from their wicked ways and turn to God, but they refuse. Here are some examples:

"Then the fourth angel poured out his bowl on the sun, causing it to scorch everyone with its fire. Everyone was burned by this blast of heat, and they cursed the name of God, who had control over all these plagues. *They did not repent of their sins and turn to God* and give him glory.

"Then the fifth angel poured out his bowl on the throne of the beast, and his kingdom was plunged into darkness. His subjects ground their teeth in anguish, and they cursed the God of

Heaven for their pains and sores. But *they did not repent of their evil deeds and turn to God"* (Revelation 16:8-10 NLT, *italics added*).

"There was a terrible hailstorm, and hailstones weighing as much as seventy-five pounds fell from the sky onto the people below. They cursed God because of the terrible plague of the hailstorm" (Revelation 16:21 NLT).

God sends a number of plagues, heat from the sun, darkness, and a brutal hailstorm so people might repent, and they curse him instead! The final blow is in the last chapter of the Bible, where a spectacular new eternal city is described for all who worship Jesus, but outside the city it's brutal: "Outside the city are the dogs—the sorcerers, the sexually immoral, the murderers, the idol worshipers, and all who love to live a lie" (Revelation 22:15 NLT). Those who are described as "all who love to live a lie" are those who persist in loving darkness rather than light, as Jesus prophesied in John 3:19-20. Loving to live a lie is to acknowledge that it is, in fact, a lie. They know who has sent the plagues. They have been confronted with the greatness of God, but they refuse and reject him anyway, and sadly, they end up in Hell.

At this point, with a heartbroken sigh, God says, "Okay, have it your way." And the whole time the Devil rejoices and whispers that his place is so much better than God's.

One other type of person is also in danger of Hell. The one who will not forgive a wrong done to them. Jesus said, "If you don't forgive others their sins, your Father will not forgive your sins"

(Matthew 6:15). Jesus spoke of this more than once. It's a huge warning that may surprise many expecting to enter into Heaven, and I believe this is one of the key ways the Devil gets people into Hell—to get them to hold on to unforgiveness and bitterness and resentment. That is his whole existence, and he wants it to be yours and mine too. It has been said that bitterness and resentment are the poison we use to kill others, but we end up drinking it ourselves.

The Devil loves it when we buy his deadly, Hell-bent elixir. The Devil lures you in and baits you with bitterness, resentment, and unforgiveness. You drink it all and you end up in Hell, and once you are there, it is for all eternity! Scary!

What is Hell Like?

Will Hell really be hot? Revelation chapters 20 and 21 make multiple mentions of a Lake of Fire. There is debate among theologians about whether this is a metaphor or actual reality. I can't say for sure.

I remember reading a depiction of hell by the author C.S. Lewis that made sense to me—here is my paraphrase: Picture a person who is bitter and resentful and self-centered at say, fifty years old. They get worse at sixty, worse again by seventy, and even more bitter and self-centered at eighty years old. It's just a downward curve until they die, and then there they are in Hell with no ability to get better—to learn grace and love. On it goes as the downward curve of bitterness continues unabated. At 10,000 years old, imagine how utterly miserable that person would be! Think of Gollum in the *Lord of the Rings,* or Emperor Palpatine/Darth Sidious in *Star Wars* (but without all the power)—just miserable, bitter, and self-centered to the extreme hideous reality of their horrible selves. If you can imagine that, now picture a whole community or city filled with nothing but those type of people. That would most certainly be a place where there would be much weeping and gnashing of teeth—a place easily described as Hell.

Is Hell real? After reading this chapter, where do you place it on Amir's scale?

A = Absolutely authentic.

B = Maybe authentic but questionable.

C = No way—pretty much all fabricated.

C.S. Lewis said, "There are two kinds of people in the end: Those who say to God, 'Thy will be done,' and those to whom God says, in the end, 'Thy will be done.'"[27] The first will be in Heaven. The latter are destined for Hell. All in Hell choose it. Without that self-choice, there could be no Hell.

One last thought: If you're a Christ-Follower, and you really do embrace the doctrine of Hell, it should provide massive motivation to do all you can to keep friends, relatives, neighbors, and any other human being from going there. That's a huge part of our mission. The alternative is infinitely so much better!

seven

Heaven

Over the years I have thought a lot of Heaven. I imagine the times we think of Heaven most is when a loved one dies. We consider what it must be like for them in Heaven, or as we contemplate about our own death, we hope to be with them again. I often think how awesome Heaven will be—in terms its beauty, what we will find there, the sheer majesty of it. I think of my favorite places on earth, like the Napali Coast on Kauai, Hawaii, the Hoh Rain Forest on the Olympic Peninsula in Washington State, the Great Barrier Reef, the mountains of Banff in Canada, Queen Elizabeth Park and the Source of the Nile on Lake Victoria in Uganda. I could go on and on.

A few places I've been were so exquisitely breath-taking that I had to pause for an hour or so and just take it in. I sensed and even said, "God has been here!" I believe the very best of this earth is but a reflection of what we will encounter in Heaven, but in Heaven, it will be even better.

Then there's the food! The great banquet that Christ describes in the Gospels is going to be the most spectacular buffet, like nothing we've ever seen or eaten! The best food ever, where we can eat all we want and not gain weight!

And the people! Imagine your very favorite person on this planet—the most loving, most fun, most humble, most creative. Everyone is going to be like that, yet in their own unique way, including you. *If...* If you believe and trust in the King of Heaven, Jesus Christ.

That's my brief take on Heaven. In my understanding, it's going to be way better than our existence on this earth in its current state, and it's certainly going to be the antithesis of Hell. But here's the question: *Is my understanding real?* What is it based upon? Is there really "a better place" called Heaven?

In the Bible, John the Apostle was given a series of visions pertaining to things to come, which he wrote down in the Book of Revelation. After the plagues and the judgment we read about in the last chapter, John is given a vision of Heaven. He writes in Revelation 22:

"Then the angel showed me the river of the water of life, as clear as crystal, flowing from the throne of God and of the Lamb down the middle of the great street of the city. On each side of the river stood the tree of life, bearing twelve crops of fruit, yielding its fruit every month. And the leaves of the tree are for the healing of the nations" (Revelation 22:1-2 NIV).

Pause a few minutes and meditate on these two verses. A river of the water of life—Life! This vision given to John shows that Heaven will be a place teeming with life, because God is a God of life. A river of life creating trees and fruit, with new crops every month, and leaves that heal every disease! It is so amazing! It's not surprising that the God of life would fill his eternal creation with life. Before this passage, in the previous chapter, John sees the most amazing sight:

> "Then I saw 'a new heaven and a new earth,' for the first heaven and the first earth had passed away, and there was no longer any sea. I saw the Holy City, the new Jerusalem, coming down out of heaven from God, prepared as a bride beautifully dressed for her husband. And I heard a loud voice from the throne saying, 'Look! God's dwelling place is now among the people, and he will dwell with them. They will be his people, and God himself will be with them and be their God. "He will wipe every tear from their eyes. There will be no more death" or mourning or crying or pain, for the old order of things has passed away'" (Revelation 21:1 NIV).

A new Heaven and a new Earth! As we wonder what Heaven will be like, it seems like it is going to be a combination of Heaven and Earth, brand new and better than before, redeemed, and full of people who have also been made new and redeemed. That makes so much sense to me because as I read the Bible, I am constantly amazed at the redemptive nature of our God. After all, His greatest act of redemption was sending His Son to the cross to redeem you and me.

This passage also tells us Heaven will be a place of pure joy and happiness—no more tears, mourning, crying, or pain. Everything is made new. It is no wonder the Apostle Paul wrote to the church in Thessalonica:

> "And now, dear brothers and sisters, we want you to know what will happen to the believers who have died so you will not grieve like people who have no hope" (1 Thessalonians 4:13 NLT).

As a pastor, I've most often quoted that passage in memorial services. Paul is saying, "Go ahead and grieve the loss of a loved one who died, but if they believe in Jesus, please don't grieve as if you'll never see them again!" There is hope! And the hope Paul is speaking of is not wishful thinking like, "I hope I win the lottery." Hope is a very real, almost tangible expectation that it will in fact happen. I have preached and shared with many people over the years that when a loved one dies or when tragedy strikes, this is precisely when we really need to believe what we say we believe.

What do you really believe about Heaven?

Have you given much thought to what you believe about Heaven? Do you really believe what you say you believe? When asked, many people say they believe in Heaven. The good news is, way more people say they believe in Heaven than in Hell. Here are some statistics:

Belief in Heaven—According to a Pew Research Poll[28]

72 percent of Americans

95 percent of Mormons

93 percent of Black Protestants

89 percent of Muslims

82 percent of Evangelicals

80 percent of Catholics

50 percent or less of Jews, Buddhists, and Hindus

Answering a poll is far different than putting your beliefs to work. I spend quite a bit of time in Africa, and here is something I have observed: Poorer nations embrace hope. Most people who live there and believe in Jesus have a very real hope in Heaven because life on this Earth is so hard. But just because we hope for it, doesn't make it real. Because this life *is* so difficult, we might be swayed by the wishful thinking of "a better place." We need to hear about Heaven from someone we can trust—so it is good to know that Jesus said a ton about Heaven. Here are a few verses:

> "In the same way, let your light shine before others, that they may see your good deeds and glorify your Father in Heaven" (Matthew 5:16 NIV).

"...that you may be children of your Father in Heaven" (Matthew 5:45a NIV).

Then in the Lord's prayer, Jesus begins with:

"This, then, is how you should pray: 'Our Father in Heaven, hallowed be your name...'" (Matthew 6:9 NIV).

There are many other Bible verses Jesus speaks about Heaven as the place where His Father is. Even though God is omniscient (everywhere), it is where God and Jesus reside. Here is another Bible verse where Jesus states God the Father really wants us there too:

"My Father's house has many rooms; if that were not so, would I have told you that I am going there to prepare a place for you?" (John 14:2 NIV).

Jesus says, "Hey, I'm going to be with my Father in Heaven. He has the most amazing place. And when I get there, I'll be preparing for your arrival. I can't wait! It's going to be so good."

The Doctrine of the Resurrection

Did he really rise from the dead? In order to truly believe in a real Heaven, we must first believe in the resurrection of Jesus. If Christ did not raise from the dead and later ascend into Heaven, then how can we know for sure that Heaven is in our future as well? The resurrection is a primary doctrine of Christianity that is intimately tied to our belief in Heaven. The Apostle Paul wrote:

"For what I received I passed on to you as of first importance: that Christ died for our sins according to the Scriptures, that he was buried, that he was raised on the third day according to the Scriptures, and that he appeared to Cephas, and then to the Twelve. After that, he appeared to more than five hundred of the brothers and sisters at the same time, most of whom are still living, though some have fallen asleep. Then he appeared to James, then to all the apostles, and last of all he appeared to me also, as to one abnormally born" (1 Corinthians 15:3-8 NIV).

Paul makes a massive statement in that Jesus rising from the dead is of "first importance!" He is saying there is *no other more important doctrine* than the resurrection of Jesus Christ. He backs up his claim by saying there are key witnesses who actually saw Jesus physically risen from the dead, including Cephas (Peter), the Twelve (disciples), then a group of five hundred people, and then James. This James was the younger half brother of Jesus who didn't believe in Jesus as Messiah until he saw him raised from the dead. Finally, Paul rounds off his list by declaring that he saw the risen Jesus as well.

What is interesting to note, even though Paul didn't include them in this particular list, the very first people who were recorded to have seen the resurrected Jesus were women. The Gospel of John records Mary Magdalene, and the Gospel of Matthew includes "the other Mary" as the first to see him and touch him. The Gospel of Luke likewise records women as the first to see him. In those days, women would not be considered credible witnesses, so why would Matthew, Luke, and John say that women saw Jesus first? If it would affect the credibility of their testimony, why not just omit that part? Because it's God's Word, and the truth is paramount. Most secular writers would have omitted it, but that's exactly what makes the Gospel writers' accounts of the resurrection of Jesus most credible—they both recorded it exactly how it happened— the women saw Jesus first.

Another passage of note is when Thomas, one of Jesus' twelve disciples, heard that Jesus had risen from the dead but didn't believe it. If you've ever heard the phrase "Doubting Thomas" used of someone who is skeptical, it originates from this very Thomas.

"Now Thomas (also known as Didymus), one of the Twelve, was not with the disciples when Jesus came. So the other disciples told him, 'We have seen the Lord!' But he said to them, 'Unless I see the nail marks in his hands and put my finger where the nails were, and put my hand into his side, I will not believe.' A week later his disciples were in the house again, and Thomas was with them. Though the doors were locked, Jesus came and stood among them and said, 'Peace be with you!' Then he said to Thomas, 'Put your finger here; see my hands. Reach out your hand and put it into my side. Stop doubting and believe.' Thomas said to him, 'My Lord and my God!'" (John 20:24-28 NIV).

There is much evidence for Christ's bodily resurrection, both practically within the biblical text, and historically based on outside sources and extra-biblical accounts. A factual resurrection is crucial to the authenticity of all Christ-followers. The Apostle Paul knew the stakes of Christ's resurrection when he wrote:

"For if the dead are not raised, then Christ has not been raised either. And if Christ has not been raised, your faith is futile; you are still in your sins. Then those also who have fallen asleep in Christ are lost. If only for this life we have hope in Christ, we are of all people most to be pitied" (1 Corinthians 15:16-19 NIV).

If Christ has not risen, then our faith, our hope, everything we believe in—everything I've written in this book so far—is a complete waste of time and energy. Our dedication to an expectation of eternal life would all be for nothing, a worthless striving by pitiful human beings! But it *is* true, which makes Paul's next words so great:

"But Christ has indeed been raised from the dead, the firstfruits of those who have fallen asleep. For since death came through a man, the resurrection of the dead comes also through a man. For as in Adam all die, so in Christ all will be made alive" (1 Corinthians15:20-22 NIV).

Christ *has* indeed been raised from the dead—it's true! As Thomas said, say with me right now: *"My Lord and My God!"* Because Jesus rose from the dead, all who put their faith in Him will rise to be with Him in Heaven.

When *do* we get to go to Heaven? Will it happen right when we die, or do we sleep in the grave for centuries before we get to experience eternal life? Jesus was clear on this point. Luke records in his gospel that when Jesus was hung on the cross, two criminals were crucified with him, one on his left and one on his right. One of these men, after acknowledging his own guilt and Jesus' innocence, pleads:

> "'Jesus, remember me when you come into your kingdom.' Jesus answered him, 'Truly I tell you, today you will be with me in paradise'" (Luke 23:42-43 NIV).

Jesus said the criminal would be with him in paradise *today!* Right now, you're alive...next minute, heart attack! (Clutch your heart for drama!) Boom! You're dead! In the blink of an eye! Do not pass Go, do not collect $200! No jail, no Purgatory, no sleeping in the grave, but Heaven...*instantaneously!*

Billy Graham, perhaps the greatest Christian evangelist who ever lived, died a few years back. While now he certainly knows for sure, this is what he believed:

> "From my own study of the Bible, I'm convinced that when we die, we immediately enter the presence of the Lord. At some future time, we will

be given new bodies, similar to the body Jesus had after His resurrection. But in the meantime, our souls are with the Lord, and we are fully conscious of being in His presence."[29]

Soul Sleep

Some have put forth the concept of the doctrine of *soul sleep*. This idea comes from when the Bible uses the term, "fallen asleep," as in 1 Corinthians 15:20 above. The way it is used is another way of saying that a person has died. It does *not* infer someone's soul is held in limbo for some period of time. The doctrine of soul sleep expresses that when a Christian dies, their soul goes into an unconscious state until Christ returns, which, depending on when you die, could be a day or thousands of years. From what we learn above in the exchange between the criminal and Jesus, we know when a Christ-follower dies they will be in paradise immediately.

What about Our Physical Bodies?

This is a great question. I have contemplated much as I read the Scriptures and have thought about what Jesus must have looked like when his disciples did *not* recognize him at first. I'll get to that in a minute—but first, what about our dead bodies?

As stated above, our spiritual souls will instantaneously be with the Lord the moment we die. However, our physical bodies will likely be in one of two states after we die: 1) Embalmed in a casket and buried, or 2) Cremated to ashes in an urn. At Christ's return,

He will reunite our physical remains, in whatever state they are in, to our resurrected spiritual bodies. At that point, our bodies will be more awesome than ever! The Apostle Paul is clear:

> "There are also bodies in the heavens and bodies on the earth. The glory of the heavenly bodies is different from the glory of the earthly bodies. It is the same way with the resurrection of the dead. Our earthly bodies are planted in the ground when we die, but they will be raised to live forever. Our bodies are buried in brokenness, but they will be raised in glory. They are buried in weakness, but they will be raised in strength" (1 Corinthians 15:40-43 NLT).

I've been asked to address the practice of cremation. Paul writes in the above passage, "Our earthly bodies are planted in the ground when we die, but they will be raised to new life." He is saying that our remains are merely a seed God will redeem for our future glorified bodies in Heaven. This understanding gives us enormous latitude. Does the body need to be embalmed? Do the dead need to be in a coffin? Does the deceased need to have on a proper dress or suit to be raised for Heaven? What about Christians who were chopped to pieces or fed to lions? What about Christians burned at the stake? Will they be admitted to Heaven? Only one thing is necessary: to believe in Jesus Christ! Ashes, a head, chewed up remains, regurgitated by lions…well, you get the point. The God who created Heaven and Earth by speaking His word can and will redeem all who have put their faith in Jesus in this life.

The point is, we will have the most awesome physical bodies in our eternal dwelling place. When Jesus rose from the dead, neither the women nor the disciples recognized him at first. The reason for this is not explained but consider this: Most theologians and historians believe Jesus lived till he was about thirty-three-and-a-half years old. He died, and then he was raised—and with a glorified body, no less! Now think about when you were at your very healthiest and best—your most "glorified" self. For me, that would be about twenty-three years old. I was young, lean, *and had hair*. Everything was working like it was supposed to and in its optimum shape! Since Jesus was a real human, he was subject to aging too. So, imagine if in his resurrected state of being he looked ten years younger. That alone would make a pretty significant difference, and could certainly explain why the women and disciples didn't recognize him at first.

Who Gets to Go to Heaven?

So many people believe there is a Heaven, but does simply acknowledging the existence of Heaven mean you get to go? Look what Jesus says:

"Whoever acknowledges me before others, I will also acknowledge before my Father in Heaven. But whoever disowns me before others, I will disown before my Father in Heaven" (Matthew 10:32-33 NIV).

"Not everyone who says to me, 'Lord, Lord,' will enter the kingdom of Heaven, but only the one

who does the will of my Father who is in Heaven"
(Matthew 7:21 NIV).

"I am the gate; whoever enters through me will
be saved. They will come in and go out, and find
pasture" (John 10:9 NIV).

"Jesus told him, 'I am the way, the truth, and
the life. No one can come to the Father except
through me'" (John 14:6 NLT).

Many years ago, I attended a church up in Seattle called University Presbyterian Church. The Pastor, Earl Palmer, was a well-known preacher and teacher of the word of God. I remember he did a series on the book of Revelation, a task I am finally engaged in as I finish this book. My concern is how often people and pastors alike get too caught up in the imagery and visions of John and often don't give the entire book the justice it deserves. Earl Palmer was different. He said something at the onset of the series that has stuck with me ever since. It went something like this: "As we embark on this series in the book of Revelation, we can get caught up in the visions and the interpretation of the visions and forget what's most important. The book of Revelation is all about Jesus, the Lord! Make sure after all the visions and imagery are interpreted that Jesus is your Lord."

That, and that alone, will ensure your place in Heaven.

Do you agree with the Bible's view on Heaven? Give it a grade on Amir's scale, but before you circle one of the following, be sure you are being objective, rather than subject to your feelings.

Where do you see Heaven on Amir's scale?

A = Absolutely authentic.
B = Maybe authentic but questionable.
C = No way—pretty much all fabricated.

Our Quest for Paradise and Immortality

We have this thing about living forever. According to legend, Alexander the Great, who ruled from 336-323 BC, explored the far reaches of the world for the Fountain of Youth and the immortality it would bring, and at one point he thought for sure he found it. In the early 1500's, Spanish conquistador and explorer Ponce de Leon sought to find the Fountain of Youth on a newly discovered peninsula of land north of the Caribbean in what is now known as Florida. Many cultures and different ethnic groups from all over the planet have sought the proverbial Fountain of Youth for millennia, obsessed with immortality. Songs are written about it. One of my favorites is "The Man Who Lives Forever" by Lord Huron. In it, the singer laments that he wants to be "the man who lives forever," and ultimately questions why our story can't "just go on forever?"[30]

What if I told you we *can* live forever? Humans are obsessed with eternity because God made us *for* eternity: "He has also set eternity in the human heart; yet no one can fathom what God has done from beginning to end" (Ecclesiastes 3:11 NIV). The evidence of this truth is overwhelming, and the search for a Fountain of Youth by so many throughout history proves the point. We long for eternal life.

Heaven is going to be great, but what happens to our loved ones who don't believe in Jesus? Some will say, "I couldn't bear to live in bliss in Heaven knowing they are in torment in Hell". Consider what God proclaimed through the prophet Isaiah some 2700 years ago: "Look! I am creating a new heavens and a new earth, and no one will even think about the old ones anymore" (Isaiah 65:17 NLT). God is declaring that Heaven will be so wonderful we won't even think about what our lives on Earth were like before. That's hard to fathom.

Sometimes we impose our current realities on what we imagine our future in Heaven will be like. We express such thoughts as: "I will never be able to be totally happy if my wife or my husband doesn't make it to Heaven, and they are suffering in Hell forever." While this kind of sentiment is certainly understandable, think of it like this: When I was in the second grade, I had a girlfriend named Bonnie. At eight years old, I was sure she was the one. I even kissed her out on the playground during morning recess. Our relationship lasted a few weeks. Some years later when I was in middle school, I remembered her as my very first girlfriend. I vaguely remembered her again in high school. Beyond that, I never really thought much about her until writing this book. Emotionally, I have become completely detached from her.

Eternity is going to make ten years or fifty years with someone seem like a day, or a few weeks at best. This may be hard to fathom now, but eternity with God is going to be so, so good that we won't give much thought to people who didn't make it, if at all. Perhaps God will simply erase all those unpleasant and painful memories. In Heaven, there will be blissful, unencumbered relationships with Jesus and all your best friends who professed Jesus. We will even get to talk to people from ancient history. We will get to know them deeply. Imagine, we'll have an eternity to get to know everyone in Heaven! I can't wait to go fishing with Peter—I love him already, he's so much like me.

Jesus loves you so much He died for your sins and mine. But more than that, He *likes* you. He likes you and me so much that He wants to spend all eternity with us. In C.S. Lewis' fantasy series *The Chronicles of Narnia*, Narnia was a magical land where animals talked and there were great adventures. It mirrored a biblical reality, where Aslan, the great lion, was the Christ figure of that world. Throughout the series, Aslan was instrumental in the overcoming of evil in Narnia, even sacrificing himself and bringing redemption into the land. At the end of the series, the final evil was a great falling away of the people in disbelief, leading to the ultimate destruction of that world. Those who believed passed through a door into a new land, a brand new Narnia, where they could remain forever. The last paragraph of the final book, *The Last Battle*, says this:

> "Their Life in this world and all their adventures in Narnia had only been the cover and title page; now at last they were beginning Chapter One of the Great Story which no one on earth has read; which goes on forever: in which every chapter is better than the one before."[31]

That is eternity with God, friends: a new Heaven and a new earth, where God is going to restore all things. Where there are no more relational rifts or pain or sorrow or death—nothing but bliss. Are you interested?

conclusion

Question: Why does any of this matter?

Answer: Because God doesn't want anyone to perish!

Whether you're a pastor, leader, church planter, or new to the Christian faith, God wants to use you to populate Heaven. He wants you to grow more in love with Him and more in love with people—all kinds of people.

Jesus is the one and only way to get to Heaven. He clearly stated this in John 14:6 when he said, "I am the way, the truth, and the life, no one comes to the father except through me." People need Jesus, and God longs to use you and me as a way to get people to Him.

Recently, I read a passage in Scripture that has always touched me and motivated my missional heart for Jesus. The story is about a wise woman from Tekoa who was sent to King David to help him reconcile with his son, Absalom. At one point in their conversation, she says to the king:

"All of us must die eventually. Our lives are like water spilled out on the ground, which cannot be gathered up again. But God does not just sweep life away; instead, he devises ways to bring us back when we have been separated from him" (2 Samuel 14:14 NLT).

The truth is all of us must die eventually. If you're a Christ-follower, your top priority should be to do everything you can to get people to Jesus and make them his disciples. He has made this our task this side of Heaven. Knowing, understanding, living out, and sharing these Basic truths of historic orthodox Christian theology is the most proven path to make that happen. Sometimes I observe people of different denominations get sidetracked by emphasizing the secondary doctrines, so much that it clouds the primary doctrines, and worse, it obscures the Gospel message of salvation in Jesus alone. I am certainly not for that. Then other times I've observed that God uses those secondary doctrines as a way to get people to Jesus. When I see that work, I am definitely for that. Just be aware that the Devil also uses the secondary doctrines to divide. So please, be careful of that.

We don't learn all these doctrines just to make us smarter or seem more spiritual—*no!* They are to help us grow and mature, to create a desire within us to love others, and devise ways to bring people back to God who are separated from Him so they can spend all eternity with Him.

This passage challenges me to stay on mission. God does not just sweep life away. His plan is to bring people to Himself. And His plan is to use you to do it.

endnotes

Introduction

1 The words "Holy Catholic Church" back then did not necessarily mean being a "Catholic" Christian when this creed was written. It simply meant, "all Christians." Therefore, I would change the word Catholic to Christian when reciting it in my Protestant church.

2 Jeru was not his real name. I changed it here to protect the guilty.

Chapter One – The Bible

3 Geisler, Norman and Ronald, Brooks. *When Skeptics Ask: A Handbook on Christian Evidences*, 159–59. Baker Books 2013.

4 Strobel, Lee. *The Case for Christ: Investigating the Evidence for Jesus*, 63. Grand Rapids: Zondervan 2013.

5 Ramsey, Sir William. "Archeology Verifies the Bible as God's Word." Christian Trumpet Sounding. Accessed October 22, 2022. www.christiantrumpetsounding.com.

6 Brucker, Brad. *Grow: Journey to a Transformed Life*. XULON Press 2017.

7   Manser, Martin H. *The Westminster Collection of Christian Quotations.* Louisville KY: Westminster John Knox Press, 2001.

Chapter Two – The Trinity

8   *Encyclopædia Britannica.* Encyclopædia Britannica, inc. Accessed October 22, 2022. http://www.britannica.com/.

9   Vitz, Paul C. *Faith of the Fatherless: The Psychology of Atheism.* San Francisco: Ignatius Press, 2013.

10 Wehnam, G.J., Motyer, J.A., Carson, D.A., & France, R.T. (editors). *New Bible Commentary*, 1266. Downers Grove IL: InterVarsity Press 1994.

11 Lewis, C. S. *The Lion the Witch and the Wardrobe.* London: HarperCollins, 2005.

12 Green, Steve, and Green, Jackie. *This Dangerous Book: How the Bible Has Shaped Our World and Why It Still Matters Today*, 115. Grand Rapids MI: Zondervan 2022.

Chapter Three – The Devil

13 Bedard, Paul. "57% Believe in the Devil, 72% for Blacks, 61% for Women." Washington Examiner. Washington Examiner, September 19, 2013. https://www.washingtonexaminer.com/57-believe-in-the-devil-72-for-blacks-61-for-women.

14 Nussman, David. "Most US Catholics Don't Believe in Devil." Church Militant - Serving Catholics, August 30, 2017. https://www.churchmilitant.com/news/article/most-us-catholics-dont-believe-in-devil.

15 Scazzero, Peter, and Warren Bird. The Emotionally Healthy Church. Grand Rapids: Zondervan, 2015.

16 The Coexist image is an image created by Polish, Warsaw-based graphic designer Piotr Młodożeniec in 2000. "Coexist (Image)." Wikipedia. Wikimedia Foundation, September 18, 2022. https://en.wikipedia.org/wiki/Coexist_(image).

Chapter Four – Sin

17 Editors. "Hurricane Irma: Where It Is Now and What We Know." USA Today. Gannett Satellite In-formation Network, September 11, 2017. https://www.usatoday.com/story/news/2017/09/10/when-hurricane-irma-move-inland/650721001/.

18 Kozlowska, Hanna. "The US Murder Rate Was Up Again-and Chicago Had a Lot to Do with It." Quartz. Quartz, September 25, 2017. https://qz.com/1086403/fbi-crime-statistics-us-murders-were-up-in-2016-and-chicago-had-a-lot-to-do-with-it.

19 Duffin, Erin. "Number of Married Couples in the U.S. 1960-2021." Statista, September 30, 2022. https://www.statista.com/statistics/183663/number-of-married-couples-in-the-us/.

20 Lewis, C.S. *Mere Christianity*, 109. New York, NY: Macmillan, 1967.

Chapter Five – Salvation

21 Boa, Kenneth. *Cults, World Religions, and the Occult: What They Teach, How to Respond to Them*. Eugene, OR: Wipf and Stock Publishers, 2012.

22 Ibid.

23 Ibid.

24 Much of this paragraph is paraphrased or quoted directly from the following three articles:

Berger, Helen A. "What Is Wicca? An Expert on Modern Witchcraft Explains." The Conversation, August 30, 2021. https://theconversation.com/what-is-wicca-an-expert-on-modern-witchcraft-explains-165939.

Worthen, Molly. "400 Years Ago, They Would Be Witches. Today, They Can Be Your Coach." The New York Times. The New York Times, June 3, 2022. https://www.nytimes.com/2022/06/03/opinion/spiritual-coaches-religion.html.

"Wicca." Accessed October 25, 2022. https://www.defenseculture.mil/Portals/90/Documents/Toolkit/ReligiousAwareness/FACTS-REL-Wicca-20191106.pdf?ver=2020-01-31-142221-557.

25   "What Is the 'Gospel' Supposed to Mean?" Christianity Stack Exchange, June 19, 2013. https://christianity.stackexchange.com/questions/16873/what-is-the-gospel-supposed-to-mean.

Chapter Six – Hell

26   Murphy, Caryle. "Most Americans Believe in Heaven … and Hell." Pew Research Center. Pew Research Center, November 10, 2015. https://www.pewresearch.org/fact-tank/2015/11/10/most-americans-believe-in-heaven-and-hell/.

27   Lewis, C.S. *The Great Divorce*. London: Collins, 2015.

Chapter Seven – Heaven

28   Murphy, Caryle. "Most Americans Believe in Heaven … and Hell." Pew Research Center. Pew Research Center, November 10, 2015. https://www.pewresearch.org/fact-tank/2015/11/10/most-americans-believe-in-heaven-and-hell/.

29   Graham, Billy. "Do You Think We Go to Heaven the Instant We Die, or Do We Sleep (or Something like That) until Christ Comes Again?" Billy Graham Evangelistic Association, July 29, 2004. https://billygraham.org/answer/do-you-think-we-go-to-heaven-the-instant-we-die-or-do-we-sleep-or-something-like-that-until-christ-comes-again/.

30   Schneider, Ben. "The Man Who Lives Forever," performed by Lord Huron. Sony/ATV Music Publishing LLC, 2012.

31   Lewis, C.S. *The Last Battle*, 184. New York, NY: Macmillan, 1956.

basic

Resources

For presentations, study guides, videos,
other church and school resources,
or to buy more copies of *Basic*, go to:

www.epichouse.church/basic

and/or email Brad at:

bbrucker@epichouse.church

Order *Basic* books on Amazon.

Made in USA - Crawfordsville, IN
23231_9781600392443
01.13.2023 1022